TEACHING ENGLISH
FOR THE
REAL WORLD

JOE NUTT

First published 2020

by John Catt Educational Ltd,
15 Riduna Park, Station Road,
Melton, Woodbridge IP12 1QT

Tel: +44 (0) 1394 389850
Fax: +44 (0) 1394 386893
Email: enquiries@johncatt.com
Website: www.johncatt.com

ISBN: 978 1 912906 95 6

Set and designed by John Catt Educational Limited

FOR CHRIS, TONY, MAGGIE, DAVID AND JOHN.

ACKNOWLEDGEMENTS

I'd like to thank Alex Sharratt and everyone at John Catt, most especially Scott James for his striking cover design and Jonathan Woolgar for all his patience, sharp eye and wisdom editing the book. I'd also like to thank Ben Williamson, Chancellor's Fellow at the Centre for Research in Digital Education at the University of Edinburgh Futures Institute, for his expert advice on artificial intelligence.

CONTENTS

PREFACE

My career splits into two distinct halves. For almost 20 years, I taught English and English literature in secondary schools; and for almost another 20 years, I've worked in business. I went from making a living out of teaching teenagers to use the English language to using it myself to earn my living in a wide range of commercial contexts. I still do. I've written several books about English poetry, including a unique guidebook for students to Milton's epic poem *Paradise Lost*, and besides writing a regular column for *Tes* for four years, I've published short stories and articles in magazines as different as *The Spectator* and *Areo*. But most pertinently for the purposes of *Teaching English for the Real World*, almost all of my business work, whichever way you look at it, has involved writing. Even speaking in a business context is often about writing because when there are millions of pounds' worth of business at stake, you don't go into the room and wing it. If you have any sense, you write it all down first...extremely carefully. I once spent an entire afternoon crafting one sentence for a particular commercial bid and am particularly proud that today, almost ten years later, it's sprinkled liberally all over my ex-employer's various websites. I've been lead writer for two different international development organisations.

This divided career has given me a rare and invaluable perspective. It brought me to a point where I realised that were I to return to the classroom now, to teach English, I would have to do it completely differently. What I now know about professional writing – all that wealth of experience I've accumulated about how the English language functions in publishing and journalism, business, academic and commercial research – means I simply could not teach the way I used to. It would be unfair on the pupils. I would not be preparing them for the real world. Yet so little has changed in exams, the curriculum, or the way people think about teaching English in that intervening period.

This book is my attempt to help schools redress that dramatic imbalance. It's not in any sense a practical teaching guide only for English teachers, full of hints and tips, lesson plans and schemes of work – although advice will undoubtedly make an appearance, if not always directly from me, from others. *Teaching English for the Real World* is a far wider consideration of what schools and English teachers should be doing if they wish to prepare secondary school children to be successful and effective users of English, in the real world of work, higher education and adult life they will all too soon enter. It's a contribution to a lively, wider debate that schools have become embroiled in ever since someone stood up in front of an audience sometime around 1998 and said, 'Why bother reading a book when you can google it?' Or more particularly as I remember it at the time, 'More information is published online in a day than Shakespeare read in his whole lifetime.' Which was exactly what I heard the managing director of a video conferencing company say around that time. I recall actually glancing around at the audience and being completely baffled that no one else appeared as appalled as I was by such a naive, ill-informed claim. As though *information* was the same as *knowledge*, or *learning* just a practical little verb and not a profoundly significant noun. Since then, I have watched arguments about what schools are for and what they should be teaching reach fever pitch in the educational world, while technology businesses offer to hold everyone's jacket, like the sneaky kid in the playground you know started it all. For all those reasons, this book should be of interest to anyone concerned about what secondary schools teach and why they teach it, and about what the UK prime minister Boris Johnson might have meant when he spoke of providing children with 'a superb education' the morning of his 2019 election victory. Above all, this is a book about what educators mean by 'levelling up'.

One reason I left the classroom all those years ago was because I could see that teaching was about to be engulfed by a tide of new technology, and rather than be on the receiving end, I decided it might be safer and more stimulating to be on the other end of the production line, trying to influence what was being sold. Detailing how long it took me to realise I was out of my depth and that the commercial and technological forces at work were both faster and stronger than anything I could muster would take a whole separate book. Since then, writers like Neil Postman, Nicholas Carr and more recently James Williams have done a far better job than I could. James Williams's book *Stand Out of Our Light* is especially insightful because he was a senior advertising executive with Google before retraining as a philosopher at Oxford, and is one of few credible figures in the new field of technology ethics. He's quite exceptional at exposing the way one small geographical feature, Silicon Valley, has impacted on all of us when he says, 'Whether irresistible or not, if our technologies are not on our side, then they have no place in our lives.'[1] And make no mistake: however glitzy the pitch, however enthralling the activity, technology is rarely, unequivocally on the side of humanity, never mind the angels.

I used to drive my youngest daughter five times a week to and from her gymnastics club close to Heathrow Airport and in the winter, when it was dark, was always amused to see a bright yellow neon light shining above one office building because the name of the company was 'Sky Net'. Not so funny now when China is busy creating the world's largest surveillance network under the same commercial name. Even less so when you discover that it's a literal translation of the Chinese name *Tianwang*, which is part of an idiom that means 'justice is always done'.

Unlike many teachers, I escaped the great data tsunami that swallowed up whole schools and careers in the last two decades in its swirling detritus of predictive software, school improvement consultancy and endless columns of impossibly untrustworthy numbers in red, amber and green. But while the worst of that may have receded, make no mistake, technology, the way it permeates almost every aspect of modern life, has a significant impact on what you do as an English teacher. It's built into every screen that demands a child's attention in those priceless early years when they first encounter books and text. It lurks in every mobile phone that every teenager carries into your classroom in their blazer pocket, however inspirational or sententious the Latin motto hiding it. It pops up the moment they sit down in front of a PC or laptop in the school's IT suite or learning centre, and an endless range of menus drop down out of the blue offering them a bewildering, bewitching choice. 'Pay attention' is a phrase weighed down with ironic possibilities when teachers as individuals in a school building are in permanent competition with a wider invisible culture that outguns them in every imaginable way.

---

1. Williams, J. (2018) *Stand out of our light*. Cambridge: Cambridge University Press, p. 100.

Small wonder, then, that so many teachers have themselves succumbed to the siren calls of the screen or virtual worlds and that the single biggest national educational event in the UK is not an educational conference or festival but a vast trade show called BETT.

I first attended the BETT Show in 2001 as an exhibitor and, having only recently left the classroom for the commercial world, was astounded at its scale and the excitement it generated. Working for a tiny organisation banished to the fringes in a booth the size of a broom cupboard, I could only look wistfully at the massive central stands that dominated the vast space. The following year, I was in a much more comfortable, medium-sized stand exhibiting for a burgeoning start-up; and a few years later, I was working for one of those major sponsors of the show with the massive central stands. Work which actually took place in an unseen backroom venue reserved only for visitors with deep pockets. Since then, I've hardly missed a year, even though I try my damnedest. I've seen it at its zenith when Microsoft, Apple and RM had huge stands manned with dozens of employees, and I watched those shrink dramatically after the 2008 financial crash before it reinvented itself more recently as an international marketplace. In 2001, you would have been pushed to find any business that wasn't based in the UK. At my last visit in 2019, there were businesses from the US, Canada, Denmark, Russia, Israel, from all over the world, intent on selling technology into the education market. Or to put it more pertinently, to compete with teachers for their pupils' attention in their workplace. It now brands itself as 'the global meeting place for education buyers', with over 800 companies exhibiting and an expected footfall of over 34,000 visitors. Glance at delegates' lanyards and you are just as likely to walk past a minister of education from Slovenia as an IT teacher from Slough.

Wellington College's popular Festival of Education and the Academies Show, both events I've appeared regularly at, pale into insignificance in comparison. Together with a few hundred other visitors at Wellington, you might hear a celebrity add to the mountain of things they think schools should be doing, or enjoy some folk music and a black sushi rice vegan wrap sitting on a bale of straw in the June sunshine, but the impact on you and those you teach is really happening elsewhere, in an exhibition space the size of an airport, east of London every January. Although my fingers are rebelling as I type even now, BETT is the real world.

If you are an English teacher and I do my job well, by the time you finish reading *Teaching English for the Real World*, you should be better prepared to deliver lessons that those you teach will forever be grateful for. If you're a school leader, or policy adviser, then I hope you'll at least be encouraged to think more insightfully about what the job should entail and perhaps even feel far better informed to participate in any discussions about what secondary schooling is for, because as long as politicians are allowed to play a leading part in how we educate our children, those discussions aren't getting any less contentious.

CHAPTER ONE
THE REAL WORLD

English in use

The first thing I want to do is to urge you to consider the complex role English usage plays on everything from the side of a bus, through explosive social media, garish slideshows and perky (but all too often vacuous) TED talks, to the hundreds of pages of research or official reports so often used as the basis for serious political policy and commercial decision making. More than three times as many people speak English as a second language than speak it as their mother tongue. It's the language of international business, which is why multinationals use it as a common corporate language and the main language of international tourism and the hospitality industry. In countries like India and South Korea, there are charitable initiatives aimed at teaching underprivileged children English to improve their career prospects. South Korea doesn't have a digital divide, it has an 'English divide'. In the real world, English is a big deal. This is one reason why I want to step away, just for this first section of the book, from the world of novels, plays and poetry, from English as art. There are more good reasons for this. Most English teachers quite rightly see their role as crucial in introducing children to great literature, and many will devote time and considerable energy to nurturing their love of fiction, drama or verse. 'The best that has been thought and said' is an ambitious vision, even when you walk into a library in a south coast seaside town left behind by international markets on a wet Wednesday in December. Where do you even start to choose a book? Yet teachers do, and they have to. Social media is full of English teachers looking for recommendations. And from there, it's all too easy to slip into actually believing you are teaching children to emulate the writers you introduce them to. One of my first surprises after leaving the classroom was hearing a textbook publisher explain that they had abandoned sending sales staff into school staffrooms with inspection copies when they discovered through market research that most of their books were purchased on the basis of only one fact: what the school had bought before. Generations of English teachers have been at the mercy of a system that positions them as the people whose job is to teach authors how to write. Authors who are imagined as individual talents like Charles Dickens or Margaret Atwood, working diligently away in isolation, pouring words onto blank sheets of paper in a bubble of artistry that has never existed. The rot sets in as early as primary school. Here is the writer for children, Michael Rosen, asked in an interview to describe the ingredients for an imaginative childhood:

> Ideally it's the space and time to play, and to participate in the arts. So play in the sense of monkeying around with other people, whoever they are, in your family grouping, or with your mates, or people younger than you, or whatever. So time for that. But also time in whatever respect to work with materials in a trial-and-error way, finding out whether things work or not, and with language. Our ability to think up new stuff.

> If children have a lot of that, then their attitude to the world is such that the world is changeable, and also that I can partici-pate in that change. It isn't just something where I go in, and I have no power. I have no rights to operate change on this world or the environment, and my job is just to take orders.

> So people who have had the opportunity to question and play and try things out and experiment, all of these part of imagina-tive behaviours, at least have a sense in themselves that the world is malleable. That they are part of a world that changes and they can be part of change. It's not just simply whether politicians tell you you can now vote on something.[2]

Putting the repellent politicising of children aside, it is nonsense to sug-gest that merely because physical, imaginative play is healthy, verbal play must be too, especially to a teacher tasked with enhancing each child's

---

2.   www.bit.ly/2xeThfO accessed 5th December 2019.

use of language in the small proportion of their waking hours available. What classroom interlopers like Rosen fail to take into account is that you need to know the rules before you can play with them. You don't sit a child down at a piano, open a sheet of music and just smile benignly while they figure it out for themselves. Far too many teachers, in primary as well as secondary schools, are seduced by this bizarre idea that they are nurturing little authors or poets. They forget that in an entire career teaching the subject, it's highly unlikely that any one of the children they teach will ever publish a book or a poem, never mind script a play. Even if they could find a theatre to stage it. I know of one minor novelist and one children's poet I taught in almost 20 years, 10 of which were in one of the most academically selective schools in the UK.

The Royal Society of Literature carried out a survey in 2019 called 'A Room of My Own', after Virginia Woolf's famous essay *A Room of One's Own,* in which she argued that 'a woman must have money and a room of her own if she is to write fiction'. They found that 'the majority of writer respondents earned below £10,000 from their writing in 2018' and 'only 5% of writers earned over £30,000 from their writing in 2018'.[3] The real world does not have a huge appetite for creative writers of anything. To argue that the emphasis in primary school should be on 'playing' with language in a 'trial-and-error way' is both statistically foolish and professionally irresponsible when almost everyone you teach will be using English regularly for very different purposes.

A leading organisation that provides professional courses for English teachers, the English and Media Centre, ran an initiative in 2019 aimed at children in their first year at secondary school called 'Just Write'. In their promotional material, they say this:

> Teaching writing, then, cannot be overly formalised. In part, it has to remain messy, room given over for experimentation, self-expression and playfulness … They will gain a real sense of the struggles that come with trying to make language behave in the way that they want it to, and of some of the unintended – often positive – outcomes that can occur.[4]

3.   www.bit.ly/2Qz2MNL accessed 6th December 2019.
4.   www.bit.ly/2QyJ6cQ accessed 5th December 2019.

It's clear from this that the creators of Just Write and its predecessor project, Let Them Loose, think like Rosen that success comes from experimentation. More importantly, what I think their initiative shows is a dramatic misalignment between what children really need from their schools and teachers and what some of their teachers think they need. However warm and fuzzy it might feel to think you may be the one to light the spark in a future Booker Prize winner, the reality is way more mundane. For every novelist or poet failing to make a living from their writing, there is an Olympic stadium full of project managers, sales teams and marketing staff who make a comfortable living from theirs.

One of the ethical mantraps social media companies either ignored or genuinely didn't see coming was the way their products would nurture a more confrontational, binary discourse. So as soon as I say we should be thinking more about the project managers and less about the poets, I know some people will instantly assume I'm advocating a wholly utilitarian educational system in which schools exist merely to feed the workforce. That is not at all what I'm suggesting and I will redress the imbalance completely later in the book. But before we get anywhere near thinking about that, I want to focus on describing that all-important real-world context in which English usage matters. And it does indeed matter. Linguists Andrew Kehoe and Matt Gee looked at over 68,000 items for sale on eBay and found that using the word 'gent's' to describe a watch instead of 'men's' meant you could sell it for an additional £40, and describing a perfume as 'authentic' instead of 'genuine' added a £13 premium.[5] Even single words, it seems, have cash value in the real world. That's even more remarkable when you consider that the difference between 'men's' and 'gent's' is really only one 'm', a 'g' and a 't'. Careless typos in your online dating profile could cost you a date, according to researchers in the Netherlands.[6] The most basic of human endeavours, procreation, is relevant to the real-world English teacher.

A recent report published by the Education Endowment Foundation, *Improving Literacy in Secondary Schools*, begins by putting things firmly in a national context:

---

5. www.bit.ly/33FUKrZ accessed 16th December 2019.
6. van der Zanden, T., Schouten, A., Mos, M. and Krahmer, E. (2019) *Impression formation on online dating: the effects of language errors in profile texts on perceptions of profile owners.* Paper presented at the conference Etmaal van de Communicatiewetenschap, Nijmegen, The Netherlands.

Young people who leave school without good literacy skills are held back at every stage of life. Their outcomes are poorer on almost every measure, from health and wellbeing, to employment and finance.[7]

The report, based on 'the best available international research', then goes on to make seven key recommendations (which I will come to later), but what is most striking about this report, given its opening concern, is that it has nothing whatsoever to do with the real world, and everything to do with persuading teachers to change their habits and practice. There is only one reference to the real world in the whole report and although it's entirely true, even that looks internally to the school and not externally to the future world which all the children who are meant to benefit from its advice will soon enter: 'The subject specific academic vocabulary of the subject disciplines differs considerably from the language students habitually use to communicate outside of the school gates.'[8]

The report argues that instead of thinking of literacy as the sole responsibility of the English teacher, a skill easily transferable across the whole range of other subjects, schools should understand that literacy is subject specific to an increasing degree as children progress through their secondary education. So far so good. It then goes on to deal with each of its seven recommendations in turn, tying them into school practice with what it calls 'vignettes of typical literacy practices across the curriculum'.[9] These are in effect just descriptions of literacy-related activities that might take place in some schools, set up as a foil for the subject disciplinary literacy advice that follows each one.

The report focuses entirely on how English is spoken, read and written, inside a range of subject-specific silos peculiar to the rarefied world of secondary schools. In spite of its no doubt sincere aim of improving the life chances of pupils by improving how their teachers work, it ignores life itself. All of the advice – the strategies and guidance offered – is pitched, at best, towards inculcating in pupils some basic scholarly skills

---

7. www.bit.ly/39dNrsD.
8. Ibid., p. 10.
9. Ibid., p. 3.

in history, science or literary studies, for example; at worst, towards the narrow requirements of a summative national exam, the GCSE. No one thinks to connect all of this literacy with how English functions outside the school walls.

There is an exquisite irony about this. Look at the report itself and you can't fail to notice the colourful, liberal use of often childishly simplistic graphics that owe their presence not to scholarly necessity but to software accessibility. Most are little better in design terms than the standard battery of clipart offered by the most common word processing software. Each of the vignettes that kick off each of the seven sections comes with the same attached panel of seven subject icons, the relevant one expanded and in colour, the others greyed out. The report is downloadable from the EEF's website as a single printable document and doesn't contain any links, but it appears as though the designer thought they were producing a web page (see figure 1)

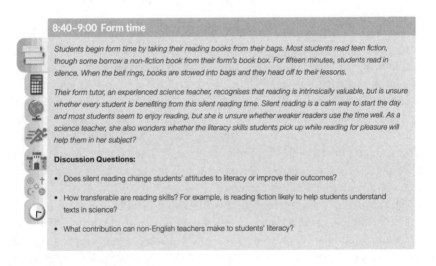

8:40–9:00 Form time

Students begin form time by taking their reading books from their bags. Most students read teen fiction, though some borrow a non-fiction book from their form's book box. For fifteen minutes, students read in silence. When the bell rings, books are stowed into bags and they head off to their lessons.

Their form tutor, an experienced science teacher, recognises that reading is intrinsically valuable, but is unsure whether every student is benefiting from this silent reading time. Silent reading is a calm way to start the day and most students seem to enjoy reading, but she is unsure whether weaker readers use the time well. As a science teacher, she also wonders whether the literacy skills students pick up while reading for pleasure will help them in her subject?

Discussion Questions:

- Does silent reading change students' attitudes to literacy or improve their outcomes?
- How transferable are reading skills? For example, is reading fiction likely to help students understand texts in science?
- What contribution can non-English teachers make to students' literacy?

Figure 1 From the EEF's *Improving Literacy in Secondary Schools*, Guidance Report, 2019, p.6. Reproduced by permission of the Education Endowment Foundation.

A small stack of books accompanies the first vignette about reading in form time; and a calculator, the second, to indicate maths. A different set of icons are associated with the seven recommendations and appear in seven colourful vertical panels to form the summary section of the report, then again once in the header for each of the sections, which are themselves colour coded. This is all clearly intended to act as an aid to reading, as though the professional teachers expected by the authors to use this material failed in their own educational careers to achieve recommendation three for children in the report itself – the 'ability to read complex academic texts' – and needed all the visual clues they could get.

That isn't the only way this report neatly illustrates my insistence in this first section that we think about English in context. The EEF prides itself on being research led, as noted earlier, using 'the best available international research'. 'Evidence' and 'evidence-informed leadership' are their thumbprints across the educational world. With UK government support, they have given birth to an entirely new kind of school, the research school, and a network exists of over 70, funded to promulgate the work of the EEF and to encourage all schools and teachers to work better, based on research evidence. It's a laudable aim.

Yet read *Improving Literacy in Secondary Schools* and you will quickly notice the way the conventional use of academic endnotes has been adapted by the authors and designers for maximum effect. Unusually, all endnote superscript references appear in bold type and rarely do the notes themselves function as conventional scholarly endnotes do (that is, to point the reader to the source of a specific and significant quotation replicated faithfully and inserted directly into the flow of the author's own discursive prose). Instead, most of them point vaguely to a range of pages in a work, and sometimes sections of considerable length. The precision that characterises all serious scholarship has been supplanted by visual rhetoric. The hefty numbered references are stamped liberally on every page after every assertion made by the authors. There isn't a single paragraph that isn't burdened with at least one. In many places, you will find not just one black and officious-looking double digit, but two or even four, lined up after one another, deployed with the same aim of trying to convince you of the strength of the evidence. Perhaps the implication is meant to be that the longer the string of bold double digits, the more compelling the evidence? This is rhetoric for the digital age.

There are also a number of interesting graphics, but I'll focus on just the one (figure 2). A large, two-dimensional image of a simplified tree (with its roots in the words 'Disciplinary literacy recognises that literacy skills are both general and subject specific') is made up of four leafy sections, each with its own matching icon and these four questions: 'How can we support children to write like geographers?'; 'How can we support children to talk like scientists?'; 'How can we support children to debate like mathematicians?'; 'How can we support children to read like historians?'[10] So, in all seriousness, what are we meant to think? The broad red page header contains another little CPD icon made up of four Legoland teacher figures looking at a whiteboard in which a smaller version of the same tree graphic is reproduced.

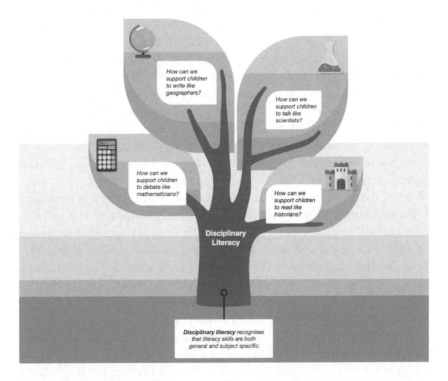

Figure 2 From the EEF's *Improving Literacy in Secondary Schools*, Guidance Report, 2019, p.9. Reproduced by permission of the Education Endowment Foundation.

10. Ibid., p. 9.

Perhaps we are meant to think about the idea of disciplinary literacy taking root and growing across the school, maybe even bearing fruit. Perhaps it's there just to reinforce something already said, a bit of helpful interleaving as it were. Either way, no one could seriously describe it as a key component of that 'complex academic text' it imagines secondary school children studying with the help of those teachers who have followed its guidance. Real-world English is full of surprises.

Now I'm not singling the EEF out here merely to cast doubt on their scholarship. What interests me is that they're not at all unusual in this respect. This kind of hybrid marketing document is common amongst lobbyists posing as researchers (and genuine lobbyists) everywhere you care to look, not just in education but in any arena where authors hope to persuade readers with information they themselves have designated 'research'. Even in isolation, the word itself gives off a powerful signal. Most significantly, it is *not* the result of evolutionary changes in scholarly practice (and remember, this is the sanctity of research evidence the EEF are talking about); it's the direct result of marketing software tools and strategies being adopted in areas that have nothing to do with product sales. It's a perfect example of how English usage is so commonly – and often unconsciously – mediated by technology. I would argue that if you're teaching English for the real world, this is exactly the kind of basic lesson children need to learn. Technology tends to constrain language use, not liberate it.

Let's turn to the report's seven recommendations themselves. I've reproduced them as a simple bulleted list:

- Prioritise 'disciplinary literacy' across the curriculum
- Provide targeted vocabulary instruction in every subject
- Develop students' ability to read complex academic texts
- Break down complex writing tasks
- Combine writing instruction with reading in every subject
- Provide opportunities for structured talk
- Provide high quality literacy interventions for struggling students

Looked at like this, as a list of tasks, they emphasise the report's introspection, its focus on what children are being taught to do – not in real life, but in school life. And that is not entirely a weakness, as later sections of this book will show. But look at the detailed advice accompanying each one and this introspection becomes even clearer. There is a distinct sense of teachers communicating with other teachers about activities that are, as it were, peculiar to schools. The discussion takes place in a school vacuum. Phrases like 'academic language' and 'specialised language' have no external reference points. It's assumed that readers will know what they mean in themselves. The whole discussion assumes everyone shares the same idea of what these refer to; but as my analysis of the report itself shows, its format, design and strategy, those external reference points matter. They matter if you are serious about teaching children a degree of genuine expertise as readers, and they matter if you are teaching children any credible skill at all as writers which they can carry with them beyond school.

Authentic writing

For as long as I can remember, English teaching has failed to confront the reality that children devote hours and hours of classroom time and homework to writing material for ostensibly no other purpose than to satisfy an individual teacher that a task has been fulfilled. How often do teachers successfully articulate a writing task in a way their pupils genuinely value as meaningful to them or their learning? I wonder: in how many English classrooms in the UK and US children are still writing newspaper reports with headlines like, 'Banquo Banquet Horror' or 'Thane Insane at Dunsinane'? Even where a teacher clearly positions such a task by spending time studying real, physical, inky newspapers at some length first (e.g. their typical layout, tone or terse paragraphing), is such an activity of value to the child – or more importantly, do they ever believe it's of value? At best, able, dutiful, responsible children will respond with a couple of A4 sides of accurate prose they have worked out is exactly what the teacher expects to see. At worst, the disaffected or hard–to–reach will waste valuable time scrawling just a line or two. No one will be improving their writing much or preparing themselves better for an occasion in the future when someone really does instruct them to write an article for a company magazine, capture what is said in a meeting or draft a press release. Because that is much more likely to be the reality than any single one of the children you ever teach actually becoming a reporter in the rapidly diminishing world of printed newspapers. If we really want their writing to improve, they need good reason to write.

I think one of the most successful lessons I used to teach is instructive here. There's nothing especially clever about it and I've no doubt lots of other English teachers have used it too, but the authentic writing model it offers is, I think, hugely important. Most English departments will do something about writing letters in the first year of secondary school. To do this, I used to first run through the formal rules, layout etc., and provide them with an example to copy. I would talk to them about the kinds of letters they might need to write in future, but end by telling them they were all going to write a specific, real letter. 'Real' in that I would provide them all with envelopes (every school office I've ever known has a heap of old envelopes) and I would deliver them. I would then ask them to choose one member of the teaching staff they liked or whose lessons or subject they enjoyed. Their task was to write a letter to that member of staff, telling them what it was about the subject or their lessons they enjoyed. The final, edited and correct versions were then put into envelopes and delivered by me to colleagues. In one very troubled school where I did this activity, a number of teachers came up to me in the staffroom, visibly touched, to say how much it had meant to them – and of course, most wrote replies without ever being asked.

What matters is that the children were never in any doubt that what they were writing had meaning and purpose for them. The difference that made to the quality, presentation and even just the length of the writing they produced was dramatic. Authentic writing should be a teacher's ideal aim for whenever they formally instruct children to commit a substantial amount of thought to paper for assessment. As teachers whose lives are inevitably bound up in one building, often just one classroom and one locality, it's so easy to fall into the trap of misunderstanding the world those we teach come from. A few years ago, after visiting Michaela Community School in West London and spending a few minutes in reception reading the impressive folder of visitors' letters, I wrote a thank-you email to the school, but also sent two printed letters, one each for the two pupils who had shown me round. I found out afterwards that one of the two had shown it to every teacher they possibly could, bursting with pride because no one had ever written to him before.

English teachers are encouraged to do all kinds of modelling activities to improve children's writing, and it's common today to find teachers using scaffolding techniques that show the child how to mimic examples at sentence level, or even lower. However effective people believe this is, it's a fundamentally flawed concept. The child isn't thinking for themselves and writing never happens without thought.

The letter lesson I've described is an effective writing lesson precisely because it gives pupils a powerful reason to think and thinking is the prerequisite to all learning. It takes away that distracting dark hole between the type of text you want them to write and the physical writing of it. The teacher who feels that their scaffolding is taking away barriers may just be making them higher. The more purposeful and valued every writing task, and the more frequently you set them this kind of work, the more likely you are to be cultivating children who really can write. Give them a convincing reason to think before you ask them to write. I'm not pretending it's easy, but the onus is on all English teachers to explain carefully and thoughtfully why they want their pupils to write something, so that as much doubt about the purpose is removed and the writers themselves feel bound to participate. There is a world of difference pedagogically between telling a class to write a poem and articulating successfully for them why such a weird, profoundly difficult task is worth the effort. Because usually, it isn't.

In many traditional boarding schools, there is no homework because no one gets to go home, but on most evenings pupils have an extended period of quiet study often called 'prep'. Short for 'preparation', the original idea was that you were given something to study which you would need for the next lesson. Few teachers ever do this today, but towards the end of my teaching career I got quite good at setting it; and at a time when far too many unhelpful voices clamour to discuss workload, I'd strongly recommend it. If you can create a situation where your pupils understand that their participation in tomorrow's lesson is actually dependent on their completing the task you set for them as homework, you're not just instilling a range of positive study habits and attitudes; you're managing your own role more effectively. University lecturer Dr Wendy Edwards took a close look at homework in her research paper 'What is the point of homework and should schools set it?'[11] One of the things she discovered looking at six different schools was that students felt that finishing off

---

11. www.bit.ly/2xmIW1m, accessed 1st January 2020.

classwork was the most common form homework took, and that the subject that gave this type of homework more than any other was…English. I'll leave you to decide what that implies about lessons that end this way.

In an article for *Tes* – 'Why grammar tests are not improving literacy'[12] – Ian Cushing, a lecturer in education at Brunel University, argued that the grammar, punctuation and spelling tests introduced as part of primary SATs exams in England in 2013 have had a damaging effect on children's writing: 'My research and that of others suggests strongly that decontextualised grammar teaching has no positive impact on writing.' He cites various teachers' dissatisfaction with teaching grammar because they believe, as he does, that it simply doesn't work:

> For example, I saw and heard about lots of writing activities that were framed like this: Write a descriptive sentence that includes one verb, two adjectives and at least three nouns. I don't think any writer would recognise this as a particularly helpful model for generating good writing. The message about language here is clear: no need to worry if it flows or if it successfully conveys the passion, concern or anger you might wish to portray. Just make sure it is packed to the rafters with a predetermined number of different grammatical elements.

You might think after my letter example that I'd be quick to agree. You'd be wrong. Cushing makes the same mistake, pointed out earlier, about the role creativity plays in primary schools. This assertion gives it away: 'no need to worry if it flows or if it successfully conveys the passion, concern or anger you might wish to portray'. What part passion, concern and anger play in the lives of most healthy seven-year-olds, I cannot imagine. Like Michael Rosen and others who have been vocal in criticising Michael Gove's reforms as backward, Cushing is overlaying an entirely political agenda onto an educational requirement.

In primary school, there is every justifiable reason to teach children a range of basic grammatical terms and structures at age seven, purely because it's valuable knowledge worth having – in exactly the same way they benefit from knowing what a season is or a fraction. There is no need

---

12. www.bit.ly/2QGy5q1, accessed 9th December 2019.

to tie it to writing at that age or even think that's your job. When they reach secondary school and subject specialist English teachers do start teaching them to write fluently, accurately and in steadily increasingly sophisticated ways, their job will be made that much easier if they are able to refer to terms like 'participle', 'infinitive' or (that favourite target of SATs moaners) 'fronted adverbial', knowing that children understand them. The mistake Cushing makes is important because it highlights again that indifference to real-world English that teachers too often exhibit. What possible reason would a seven-year-old have to write with passion or concern about anything that would have purpose or meaning to them, unless it was the leading role they didn't get in the post-SATs musical? The progressive urge to think of all primary children as nascent artists – or worse, activists – is just another example of a modern and liberal tendency to eradicate childhood altogether.

If you want to teach young teenagers to write well then you need to think empathetically about them and their world. Politicians, policy makers, lobbyists and indeed a substantial proportion of the teaching profession forget that school, for most children, is actually about friends, not lessons. This is one reason I am keen in my work for the think tank Cieo to see a more informed policy discussion about schooling and one less fixated on education. Genuinely good schools are just as much breeding grounds for healthy, positive relationships and experiences as they are effective tools for knowledge transference. This is why bullying has such a strong grip on the cultural imagination because it's a potent symbol of weak schooling. Its scars last. Bullying – the real thing, not the name calling or petty playground fisticuffs so often misnamed – is a particularly rare, individual psychological condition that only flowers in a weak school, or sub unit within a school. In good schools, it's cultural anathema and is effectively weeded out by peer pressure as well as by teachers (something I'll turn to later when discussing the effect technology has had on our culture).

That focus on friendships has implications for the writing tasks we design for children. How much more thoughtful (and therefore productive of good prose) are they likely to be if asked to write about those things that do preoccupy them, like friendships and family, rather than about adult formats and themes in which they have no natural interest like newspapers or travel brochures? I've often asked myself why secondary schools don't make diary writing compulsory in year 7. Consider for a moment the difference from the child's point of view between being handed by their school, at the start of their secondary career, a thin, anonymous, ephemeral exercise book with a pastel blue or pink cover for all their English writing and being given the gift of a substantial, hard-backed formal diary with sufficient space to last a year, maybe even longer, that they are told is their personal property for life. The idea of writing a diary has repetition inbuilt. By its very nature as a recording device, it provides a reason to write that, like the letter example I gave earlier, reduces, if not removes entirely, the doubt and hesitation that usually comes between your instructions and their physical transcription. It gives them reason to think.

Some of you may have had a child like my youngest daughter, for whom a diary became a profoundly precious, personal companion. My daughter called hers Kat. I've no idea why, but from the age of about eight she has been a committed, if (like most) intermittent diarist, writing usually before she goes to sleep and often at great length. I've no doubt whatsoever that what was to her an entirely real and personal activity contributed substantially to her impressive writing performance across all her academic subjects.

What I'd like to stress from this is how important it is for English departments and teachers to question the value of the written tasks they devise for the teenagers they teach. I'm not prescribing specific ideas like diary writing because I can point to credible research evidence that they work better than others. I've spent far too much time working on educational research for all kinds of clients to have much faith that such a piece of research could be devised anyway. I am encouraging you to work backwards from the real world of English into the classroom and to think more about why those you teach might want to write anything, and less about those conventional English language tasks that fill up those pink and blue exercise books rather more slowly and with far less enthusiasm, energy and accuracy, than my daughter filled her numerous volumes of Kat.

I'm saving most detailed discussion about technology specifically for the final section, but it's appropriate here, when discussing writing, to sow the seed of an idea. I think I'm skating on glacially thick ice to say that the most important things teenagers in contemporary classrooms in the UK and US write today, as far as they're concerned, are typed onto the small screen they carry around in their pockets all day. As adults and teachers, we get to decide if that's educationally a good thing or a bad thing – and more significantly, what to do about it. Shirking this responsibility is no longer a professional choice, if it ever was. Unlike most of its critics worldwide, I've actually been to Michaela School in West London and understand completely why its headteacher Katharine Birbalsingh and others have a draconian policy on mobile phones. I was still teaching full time when mobile phones first started to appear in those teenage pockets and recall having a conversation with the chap who was then the headmaster of the school in which I taught and advising him to institute a ban immediately. He thought differently. Within weeks of our conversation, he was suspending a normally polite pupil because they had refused to give their phone to a colleague – and within months, I had decided to work elsewhere.

Where writing really happens – mobile phones and social media

Mobile phone ownership provides schools with the ideal reason and timing to start discussions with children about real-world English because it also marks their initial encounters with social media and the serious risks associated with a life lived partially online. Imagine for a moment teaching English before the advent of mobile phones. Some readers may not have to. Imagine that all the youngest teenagers you were teaching – not the young men and women who take GCSEs but those immature year 7s and 8s – spent hours almost every day reading and writing material which was read then published instantaneously by adults in another country, entirely unknown and largely inaccessible to you, which is essentially what is happening every day they use any one of many thousands of applications on their phones. Figures about teens and their technology use vary according to the interested party commissioning the research, but I've plumped for some PISA figures because the OECD's most recent PISA report has just been published as I write and because they are an organisation teachers will know. This is from a report they published in 2018:

> In 2015, a typical 15-year-old from a country that is a member of the OECD had been using the internet since age 10 and spent

more than two hours every weekday online after school, and more than three hours on a weekend day.[13]

So that's roughly 16 hours a week. How many hours a week do you teach them English? Statistics from the US published by the Pew Research Center on internet and technology, also in 2018, pose the problem rather more starkly: 'Half of teenage girls (50%) are near-constant online users, compared with 39% of teenage boys.'[14]

The point, of course, is that before these new technologies appeared, teachers, and one hopes parents, would have been outraged at the idea that their children were embroiled in an adult, commercial world made of text and images they knew nothing about, in such an overwhelmingly time-consuming way. It's imperative that teachers take this into account when teaching English today. If the lessons you design and deliver ignore this reality, then can you honestly say you are giving these young adults the knowledge and skills they need to work and live successfully beyond the school gates?

Lessons about social media do not belong in a PSHE or citizenship classroom. They belong in the English department because even the quirky, gif-ridden world of Instagram is about communication and the language pupils use matters. I can understand if this alarms English teachers, because the moment you start to investigate social media platforms, online tools and phone apps, the scale of the problem looks daunting. If you've only just weaned yourself off a bad Amazon or Tinder habit and have no idea what TikTok or Whisper is, then you might not feel best placed to teach others; but this is not about technical proficiency or even familiarity. Technology moves so fast that those two products will already be old hat by the time anyone reads this. At a conference (in Turkey of all places) around 2009, when the latest techno hype meant sticking an 'e' on the front of everything – as in e-university, e-learning and being e-ready, as though Silicon Valley recruited all its marketing directors from Yorkshire – I actually got a standing ovation from the hall for pointing out to the hundreds of school and university teachers present that they would never be e-ready because no matter how much

---

13. OECD Publishing (2018) *Children's and Young People's Mental Health in the Digital Age.*
14. Pew Research Center (2018) *Teens, Social Media & Technology 2018.*

money they spent on kit and CPD, new products would always outstrip them. This isn't about being up to speed. It's about risk and responsibility.

In *Stand Out of Our Light,* James Williams points out the broader cultural and political dangers this new wave of technologies has imposed on an unknowing and naive public. At a time when there are teachers who believe it's professionally appropriate to encourage those they teach to miss school to attend climate change demonstrations, he says this:

> Future generations will judge us not only for our stewardship of the outer environment, but of the inner environment as well. Our current crisis does not only come in the form of rising global temperatures, but also in our injured capacities of attention. Our mission, then, is not only to reengineer the world of matter, but also to reengineer our world so that we can give attention to what matters.[15]

Encouraging children to pay attention to what matters is essentially a linguistic endeavour. If you can't decide what is and is not worth paying attention to, whose words have value and whose not, then the risks are not just obviously political, they're personal. At the time of writing, we are caught up in the most unpleasant, deceitfully conducted and downright dangerous general election I have seen in my lifetime in the UK. I'm far from alone in expressing that view. Not since the days when I walked to work every day through the City of London, nervously aware of every parked vehicle because of the IRA's bombing campaigns, have I felt so personally vulnerable. The City was cordoned off during that period with armed police and huge metal checkpoints on the major routes in. Neither were things a British citizen expected, or wanted to see, on their streets.

One of the most glib and pernicious maxims of the arcane, academic feminist movement is the phrase 'the personal is political'. It gets wheeled out by every overtly politicised individual in defence of all manner of otherwise unpalatable, indefensible, entirely political desires. It is a lie. Politics actually occupies a tiny space in most people's world views. Friends and family, employment and personal passions take up far more space than the specious policies, petty hatreds and flagrant prejudices

15. Ibid., p. 145.

that are too often the hallmarks of contemporary political life. This is of course what happens when people are not good readers. My Twitter time-line this past few weeks has been crowded with video clips of protestors carrying placards and banners plastered with terse, aggressive demands written in English, shouting the same phrases and slogans that signal nothing more edifying than their limited attention span and unwilling-ness to read. Because a true reader – someone who, as they turn the page, is actively engaging with the thoughts and ideas of the author because they want to know what *they* think; someone who has read extensively and judiciously to accumulate knowledge – knows that sophisticated problems aren't resolved with crude marketing techniques.

Tying English to the real world in the case of social media means making that all-important connection for the children between their words and the way they will be perceived. Mainstream society is still battling with this one and the reason some of these platforms can be so depressingly unpleasant places to inhabit is because far too many adults (in spite of their education, not because of it) fail to make this connection. They are often fooled by promises of privacy, they may be passionate advocates of free speech, or they may just be naive, but the common factor is failing to make a rational connection between the words they type into a keyboard and the way those very same words may be read by others. I was once astonished to find a business email I had sent years ago appear on the screen in front of me for anyone to access and read. When I wrote it, the idea that it would ever be visible to anyone other than the recipient would have been unthinkable. Luckily it was an entirely mundane sales communication; but the shock and the lesson it taught me was something else.

All good writers know that when their words are finalised in black and white, either printed on physical paper or just uploaded onto a remote server somewhere, that's it. There is absolutely nothing they can do to change the way a reader will interpret them. Genuinely skilful writers – and let's not forget this entire discussion is about how to teach children to write well – know that the words have a life of their own the moment they are released into the world and that everything significant has to happen on the page or screen before that moment. They know their own and others' editing skills matter. They know that fine tuning their prose is every bit as important an activity as their original, imaginative creativity and thinking. They know that they cannot stand over the shoulder of every reader in the world and point out things they missed or answer their questions. Write well and most people will understand you. Write badly and don't be surprised when they don't.

When I decided to write a guidebook for students to Milton's magnificent epic poem, *Paradise Lost*, I did so because I knew from my teaching experience that most teenagers find it an intellectual Eiger to climb because their education does not equip them with the background reading (what teachers today would recognise as cultural capital) to read the poem successfully – which roughly equates to understanding and enjoying it. I invested a huge amount of care and thought into both plugging that cultural capital gap and nurturing their pleasure in the poem. I had no idea whether it would work and had plenty of doubts, knowing how pedantic the world of Milton scholarship is. (If you think Shakespearean scholars are picky then you've never met a Miltonist.) So I was genuinely delighted when a reviewer in the *Milton Quarterly* made this particular comment: 'Nutt excels at looking at the poem over his audience's shoulder, so to speak.'[16]

I could not have wished for better confirmation that I had done the job I set out to do and done it well. I could sit back, relax and let the words do the job. That's how every skilled writer should feel after everything they write has been published. It's as true for the project manager as it is for the poet. If you can inculcate that same measure of achievement in those you teach, you really will be helping them as users of the English language outside those school gates.

Real-world writing involves other people

Make no mistake: real-world writing is rarely as straightforward as it might seem from the isolation of a classroom. One of the most difficult lessons to learn as a professional writer is that editors and even copy editors are also perfectly capable of wrecking your work. I've had articles published that are almost unrecognisable from the work I submitted. I've had a joke that relied on the word 'byte' expunged because a copy editor (or more likely a bit of software) changed it to 'bite', which was

---

16. Anderson, David J., (2012) 'Joe Nutt: *A Guidebook to Paradise Lost*', *Milton Quarterly*, Volume 46, Issue 4, Blackwell Publishing, p.243.

especially unfortunate because it was the punchline of the whole piece. I've had an essay wrecked because a copy editor standing in for the editor, who was on holiday, took out the opening sentence, which set the tone for the entire piece and without which I was laid wide open to criticisms that would otherwise have been impossible. I've had a major piece of research rewritten by a new, more complaint external author because my employer didn't like my findings. On one occasion, a piece I wrote for a national newspaper provoked a call to my then CEO from someone in the Education Secretary's office, who threatened to withhold all future government business. The most difficult to handle of all, in almost every context I can think of – business, research and creative – are those people commissioning the work who would actually prefer it if you wrote what *they* think. This is a profoundly difficult issue because it cuts right to the heart of what it means to write, to express your*self* in words. I imagine most English teachers would regard that as a given. The idea that, in all those writing activities they set in the classroom, they were not encouraging children to express *themselves* would be odd to say the least, even unprofessional. It harks back to that fantasy image of Dickens and Atwood working away in a bubble of creative artistry, which is what really fuels so much advice to English teachers from experts.

Yet here is a simple illustration of that. If you insist on asking a child to write a newspaper report or magazine article then don't waste your time and theirs assessing their headline, because in the real world writers *never* get to write the headlines. The publication does that for its own reasons. The internet has coined the term 'clickbait' to indicate something designed purely to make a viewer click that mouse button and headlines often fall into that category. Therefore, thinking that a 'Banquo in Banquet Horror' headline is worth rewarding with an oversized complimentary tick might seem like a good idea but it really isn't. (Unless by some miracle the child author ends up as a sub editor.)

Even in what you might imagine is an entirely pragmatic context, business writing, you will find people senior to you will want *you* to write what *they* think. Occasionally this is fair enough when the goal is more business. Until I started working for a technology company, I had no idea that literally tonnes of business writing is necessary merely for businesses to win business. This is the specialised world of commercial bidding. A huge amount of spending comes from national governments and all kinds of businesses bid for this in rigidly controlled procurement exercises that are prescribed by national and sometimes international law. Put very simply, whether you win business or not is often a matter of how well your employees can write because it's the writing that is formally assessed and indeed scored by the public sector procurers. The public sector body procuring the service or product drafts a set of complex questions, technical and commercial, which all the competing companies must respond to by a fixed deadline. These can be ridiculously complex documents. They do this through several stages, whittling down the number of businesses competing until they usually choose one of three finalists. Each time, they publish the criteria and scoring for every question. People who do this work often talk about 'answering the exam question' because it's a very useful analogy. They really are trying to score more points than their competitors in exactly the same way every child in a norm-referenced GCSE examination is in reality trying to outperform every other child.

They restrict the use of imagery, graphic and merely marketing material, and in my experience of doing this kind of work for many different companies over many years, unless the process allows you to develop a relationship with the procurement team, which it rarely does, pretty much everything comes down to those rows and rows of words on a page. It really is all about the writing – almost. The reading counts too. On one occasion, a series of bids I worked on contained essentially the same list of questions, one of which I quickly realised was gibberish. It made no sense at all, not grammatically, semantically or even, though I assure you I tried, metaphysically. It was my job to answer this question, so I wrote something roughly along these lines: 'This question makes no sense at all, so let's not pretend it does. Instead, we think this is the question you should have asked and here is our answer.' The maximum number of points for this question was 6. When the scoring came back, we'd scored 7.

In the days before electronic submissions, I once drove with my bid manager to an office block in South London with 18 cardboard boxes full of bid documents we were required to submit. I could just about carry one box at a time. Thankfully those days of in-house printing and page turning into the early hours before a deadline are over; but for so many businesses, what they write still determines whether they stay in business or not.

Let's return to the idea that people senior to you will want you to write what they think. The penultimate stage in any commercial bidding process usually involves several senior figures in the company reviewing the bid document and commenting. Often this is helpful and they spot things with the fresh eye and experience that are necessary; but it's also true that, as in the case of the media world, they can easily fall into that trap of wanting *you* to write what *they* think. It takes some diplomacy and tact to stick to your guns. It's not unusual to see documents go through review stages when one set of reviewers simply undoes changes the previous set of reviewers made. At this stage of my career, I'm in the fortunate position where I'm usually the one the final reviewers turn to.

What this all means for the English classroom is that it's crucial to instil in children the principle that writing always involves negotiating with other people. This runs counter to the way English teachers are trained and every English department's routine way of working I have ever seen. The myth of the solo creative writer driven by passion, concern and anger (or indeed any other emotion school interlopers care to choose) I highlighted earlier is just that: a myth, as fanciful and misguided as learning styles or Bloom's taxonomy. I was trained to teach English at the University of Warwick after studying for a master's in English there. It was then considered one of the best teacher training schools in the UK (and still is), so I had a quick look at what they have to say about teaching English today. They quote a head of English on their website aimed at potential trainees:

> I feel so utterly privileged to teach English. To be paid to talk about love, life, imagination, psychology, humanism, character … the list goes on. I love it when you can open students' eyes, often for the first time, to new ways of thinking about life. When you see students understand how literature and language are the fabric and mirrors of life itself. Those are amazing moments.[17]

I will leave you to reflect whether or not that sounds like they are interested in training English teachers for the real world.

---

17. www.bit.ly/2vQC1xm, accessed 12th December 2019.

Teaching English – not politics

Whatever you conclude, that head of English's idealistic vision of teaching English does invite us to think about some of the more profound aspects of the job. Free speech is the foundation on which Western democracy was built and therefore the target of everyone who seeks to overthrow it. Benjamin Franklin knew this, even as he was founding a nation, and it remains as true today as it was when the risks of failure for a nascent government must have seemed imminent and frightening. Free speech has been under renewed attack in recent years from within and without, even in nations that have regarded themselves as secure democracies for centuries. Critics of free speech are never friends of democracy. When an individual, however politically powerful or celebrated their status, attacks the voting integrity of any other individual, however virtuous they think their motive, however better informed they think their personal choice, they are no democrat. All votes weigh the same in a faithfully democratic nation, in spite of the cash thrown at them or the ignorance they stem from. That's why chartists and suffragettes died, and why ballots are secret.

At a recent conference at the Royal Society in London (where I was speaking and going over the research that argues schools are not engines of social mobility), I was saddened but not surprised by something a delegate who managed to commandeer me over lunch for a video interview told me. She explained that there was a senior financial adviser, closely connected with government in her home country, who was now openly suggesting the state abandon universal education because most ordinary citizens were too stupid to be voters. The country? Russia, a country that has never known democracy in its entire history and which has only recently managed to shake off almost a century of crippling communism. Old soviets die hard. Yet even here in the West, the idea that universities, places dedicated to the sharing of old and new knowledge for centuries, should become places where students and their teachers screen out specific speakers or ideas is only one of many warning signs that democrats should respond to. It was a key reason I wrote a lengthy essay for *Areo* magazine in 2018, '*Areopagitica* for Millennials', which sought to make John Milton's famous defence of free speech accessible to a generation of young students clearly unfamiliar with its historical importance, its argument and its inspired brilliance.

Areopagitica is one of history's greatest attacks on the urge those in power so easily develop, to censor the voices of those they govern. That urge has reared its grotesquely ugly head once again and the onus is on those of us who recognize it for what it is to decapitate it as ruthlessly and brutally as Milton and his fellow regicides dealt with the king they loathed.[18]

If teaching English is about anything, it's about teaching children to speak freely and without fear. I've no doubt that many teachers would find nothing to disagree with in that, yet be wholly unaware that in their own teaching, specifically their choice of contemporary texts, they are often doing something else entirely. Teaching a child to think and speak for themselves is incompatible with teaching a child that this particular novel, or that particular play, is important and worthy of study because it subscribes to any one political ideology. Take an objective look at the more modern texts exam boards choose and ask yourself this one significant question: why was it chosen? The mere fact that it's a recent publication means it can't be that it has stood the test of time and is widely accepted as canonical, or culturally significant. Even *The Handmaid's Tale* isn't there yet. In the unedifying aftermath of Jeremy Corbyn's electoral failure in the UK, there were teachers on Twitter seriously suggesting they needed to improve their teaching of *An Inspector Calls*. There is a well-publicised attempt by some to 'decolonise' the curriculum, which, besides the inhumane, destructive, Maoist urge to start again, is nothing more than a crude attempt to politicise the curriculum. You can't teach English without teaching history. If you cannot justify teaching a work of literature to school children, at the very least on aesthetic grounds, on its acknowledged contribution to the world's library, then should you be teaching it at all? Choosing a book for children to read because it conveys a political message you approve of isn't English teaching; it's proselytising.

In a poll carried out by *Tes* in the run-up to the recent UK general election, 60% of all teachers were supporters of Jeremy Corbyn's version of the Labour Party – only the second political party in Britain ever to be formally investigated by the Equality and Human Rights Commission

---

18. www.bit.ly/3dr808k, accessed 12th December 2019.

for racism, in this case specifically antisemitism, its infamous predecessor being the British National Party, Britain's post-war, party political version of out-and-out fascism. The left-leaning tendencies of the teaching profession have been a problem for as long as I remember, not least because professionals themselves have always turned a blind eye to the resulting and bizarre imbalance. In my early years as a teacher, conferences and professional events I attended were openly politicised and so frequently dull and dire as a result that I stopped going. There was simply nothing about teaching English, or indeed about teaching anything, to learn from them. It's not that long ago, perhaps three or four years, that I attended the national conference for state school governors held in East London and had to endure one union official and academic after another preach politics and not education. Invited to discuss English teaching at the University of Exeter earlier this year, at a conference organised by BERA,[19] I thought for a moment I had gone back in time when one teacher trainer launched the same hackneyed, unrestrained politicised attack on government policy. What's important about all of these examples, where individual politicians are targeted and derided, is the assumption that this is an acceptable way for professionals working in education to behave. If the alignment of so many teachers with what has turned out to be little more than an antisemitic cult, rejected in a spectacularly definitive manner by the British electorate in December 2019, hasn't convinced you this extreme imbalance is no longer tolerable, what would? It is never an English teacher's (or any other kind of teacher's) job to encourage those they teach to hold a specific political view. If I had any say in the matter, I would make sure this was embedded as a significant requirement in government teaching standards, not merely some lukewarm afterthought.

Here is something from the English and Media Centre again, an organisation that describes itself as 'an independent educational charity with a national and international reputation as a Centre of Excellence'. Their five aims and guiding principles include these three statements:

- 'We seek to develop our radicalism for new times and new generations of teachers.'

---

19. The British Educational Research Association.

- 'We seek to make a contribution to other areas of the school curriculum and to bring our skills and expertise to projects that benefit the community beyond formal schooling.'
- 'We are committed to addressing issues of cultural diversity and equal opportunities and seek to address the needs of students with a range of abilities.'

I should point out that this is an award-winning organisation that offers professional development courses for English teachers and that aims 'to develop and disseminate best practice and innovative approaches to language, literature and media, in all their forms. We support teachers in raising attainment and helping their students to become confident, articulate, critical, creative readers, writers, speakers and listeners for the 21st century.'[20]

I'm not sure what 'radicalism' has to do with English teachers' professional skills and knowledge or why any English teacher should concern themselves with 'equal opportunities' or 'cultural diversity' (any more than any other concerned citizen) unless they believed these entirely political goals were in some way integral to the job of teaching English. Similarly, why would 'projects that benefit the community beyond formal schooling' play a significant part in a job, which they state in their own aims is in essence about helping school students 'to become confident, articulate, critical, creative readers, writers, speakers and listeners', unless the job was in some way a political project?

Here is an extract from a recent article published by the higher education think tank HEPI that addresses this damaging political imbalance in the education sector more widely:

> There is no need to detail the widely reported incidents of 'wokeness' in higher education, newsworthy precisely because they seem strange or ridiculous to outsiders, to know that universities are marching to a different tune to many of their fellow citizens.[21]

---

20. www.englishandmedia.co.uk/about, accessed 13th December 2019.
21. www.bit.ly/2UEQuEK, accessed 16th December 2019.

The author Simon Goldsworthy, himself a university academic, explains in clear terms how this damaging imbalance comes about, and in doing so adds weight to the entire rationale behind *Teaching English for the Real World.*

> Uniquely, academics are often people who have spent their entire conscious lives in one environment: education. After ascending the different tiers of study, from school to university, they seek permanent jobs in higher education. Their experience of the outside world is therefore often limited. The world they inhabit, particularly in the humanities and social sciences, can also be rather introspective. They are appointed to their jobs and promoted by, and socialise and indeed frequently mate with, people who often share the same rather restricted experience of the world.

Most teachers take a similar route, which I would argue is a key reason we need to realign the teaching of English with the real world, with how English is used, valued and exploited there. Schools and teachers so often think of themselves as outward looking, inspirational and liberal in the broadest sense, when they are literally, in *effect*, quite the opposite, since so much of what they do has no bearing on the real world. There is one aspect of the English classroom that I think presents the ideal mechanism to teach children all about free speech and why it's something they must treasure as well as nurture in others.

In the last few years, I've been invited on several occasions to be a judge in the Debating Matters competition, a national event for sixth formers in UK schools organised by the Academy of Ideas. I'm always impressed by the calm, reasonable level of debate, something which the organisers work hard to nurture and which owes a lot to their insistence on competitors following well-established debating conventions. I've talked to competitors and the teaching staff who bring them along, and it's noticeable that these tend to be individual enthusiasts, teachers who believe debating has a significant role to play in secondary schooling and who are prepared to support it with their own time and energy. Put aside the grotesque media bear pit that is Prime Minister's Questions, and law making in the West still proceeds via formal debate. If you ever watch a parliamentary debate, you can't fail to notice just how formal and unusually disciplined it is. Debate, more broadly discussion, is really the lifeblood of commercial, cultural and political life. It's a core activity for many working adults that impacts on their personal and wider organisational success, yet it sits well down the pecking order on the curriculum for most secondary schools, if it finds a place at all. Many English teachers will run the odd classroom debate, perhaps even teach and embed the conventions, but it's more often than not an adjunct. Today, it should be core to the whole English experience for pupils because if you put parliamentary debate aside and think about where political debate is taking place today between ordinary citizens, then it's quite clear we have a problem.

The new phenomenon of lives lived partially online has meant there has been an explosion in exchanges of views and ideas that before the internet only took place in the workplace, round the family dinner table or in the pub. Millions of otherwise sane adults now voice their political views on their personal Facebook pages, in between shots of the cat and what they had for dinner last night, as though in some magical way, doing so will definitely influence other people equally busy posting pictures of cats and pasta. Others vent their passions or hatreds in tiny explosions of prose on Twitter, hoping that, like the celebrities they follow, their voice might carry. Professional journalists and politicians worry about the impact of 'fake news' or promulgate it themselves, because this revolution in technology has come so fast and so furiously it's hard to know the difference between a punch to the face or someone accidentally walking into an outstretched arm, as the BBC's political editor, Laura Kuenssberg, found out to her cost during the 2019 UK general election. Ms Kuenssberg had to retract a tweet in which she had reported the incident as a punch when video captured on a bystander's phone showed it was nothing of the sort. Video technology is now sophisticated enough to produce a convincing canine version of Riverdance or put lies into anyone's mouth. Trust is in short supply, which of course means its value has increased.

Real-world skills

English teachers must be the ones introducing children to this new, uncertain world so that they become both better consumers and better producers of the English language. If you are yourself a consumer of broadcast news or current affairs, ask yourself how often have you heard or seen a genuine exchange of views take place? How often in what might even be billed as a televised 'debate' or 'discussion' programme is there any evidence that participants are eager to hear others' views and engage in an exchange that is genuinely informative or that refines everyone's thinking? Good English teachers will regard this as a bedrock feature of their work. A skilled English teacher doesn't just listen and respond; they entice and invite further discussion, they involve more individuals and nurture a classroom disposition where everyone feels they can speak and be heard, without fear or favour, gradually adding to the knowledge of everyone in the room. Yet do they ever articulate that vital connection with the outside world of Facebook and fraud, of near anarchic English?

In the commercial world, this kind of genuine, informative discussion is crucial to success. There are countless opportunities in business for people with different skills to come together, exchange information and ideas, in order to develop something that benefits the business as a whole. It's a cliché to talk about time wasted in meetings, yet many prudent businesses have policies and strategies to make them as productive as possible. But even the most imaginative won't succeed unless employees can actually listen to what is said and add to it themselves. We progress by collaborating. I've sat through hundreds of business meetings, in dozens of companies, and they are never quite the same. Different businesses have different cultures and processes, but they all rely on the same principle that everyone taking part can speak effectively for themselves. To illustrate this, here are two examples of what happens when that principle is undermined.

In one large meeting I took part in, three companies that were collaborating on a commercial bid came together. This was an unusually large meeting, with bid teams from all three businesses present. There were perhaps 15 or more people in the room. Three people from one of the companies sat on the window ledge and, in spite of the bid manager's repeated invitations, refused to sit around the large central table set up specifically to facilitate discussion. The meeting proceeded nonetheless, but that initial signal given out by the trio effectively sabotaged the entire process that went on for months, and unsurprisingly, the final bid document, when it was produced, contained poor-quality, begrudging material from the ledge-sitters. It might sound bizarre, even childish, but the reason for this was because the trio came from a huge British business and felt they should have been leading the bid and not working under another organisation. Even though the lead organisation was a large multinational with a global reputation. Company cultures are not always healthy. On one occasion when I was joining a new employer and had some customer service training with a corps of other new recruits, we were all asked to name a company we had had a terrible experience with as a customer. Surprise, surprise, everyone who sat around my table, including me, named the ledge-sitters.

The second example concerns attending another unusually large meeting at the company I then worked for. It was to kick off some new business development activity, and when I sat down, it was immediately clear to me that I was one of the oldest present and that most were recent graduates. The meeting was led by a senior figure in the company and sticks in my mind because it really was a unique experience. In spite of the manager stressing at the outset that this meeting was collaborative and that he wanted to hear as many ideas as possible, after half an hour or more he was still waiting and it was becoming uncomfortable for everyone. Remember those excruciating seminars as an undergraduate when no one ever talked and your lecturer just sat there and waited in stubborn silence? The ex-teacher in me decided to intervene, so I offered something myself and then invited one of the young graduates present, who I knew was quite confident, to give their opinion. From then on, I led the meeting as discreetly as I could, and within a short time it had become productive and positive. Several people sought me out afterwards to thank me, and it became clear they had been intimidated by the presence of that particular senior manager and, without my intervention, would never dared to have offered an idea or opinion because they felt the career risk was too high.

Progressive educators would no doubt argue that both of these examples highlight the importance of teaching 'interpersonal' or 'soft' skills; but whatever you like to call them, they were both essentially linguistic challenges. Success or failure hinged predominantly on the choice and the quality of the language used. Nothing progressive about that.

That is true almost everywhere you care to look beyond the school gates, and even inside them if you're an employee. Teaching healthy, collaborative, discursive habits and practice as a core part of the English curriculum seems to me a contemporary imperative. Listening, in this sense, is every bit as important a skill as speaking because if you don't hear what someone says, how can you add to, refute or build on it? When was the last time you taught a lesson dedicated to effective listening? Have you ever even seen a lesson which had that as its aim? Surely a lesson or series of lessons that had that aim would serve your pupils better than one looking at unusual narrative voices or authorial point of view? I recently came across an anthology of key stage 3 material about narrative voice which contained no less than 80 extracts from novels and short stories. More evidence, if it were needed, that English teachers are far too often behaving as though their job is to nurture future novelists.

The importance of listening was something I stressed in my last book, *The Point of Poetry*, and when I'm invited to speak about it at professional conferences or just in schools, I actually include a couple of unusual audio clips before reading any verse aloud to try to jolt my audience into a new place where what their ears are doing actually matters. If you can't listen, you can never enjoy poetry.

At a time when UK teachers are being encouraged by the schools inspectorate, Ofsted, to audit their entire curriculum provision, it might be wise to ask who you might want to do that for. If you do it for Ofsted, how different in substance is it from the child who dutifully writes that news story on *Macbeth* they know the teacher wants, irrespective of its value to themselves? In its recent rethinking about curriculum, Ofsted has talked a lot about what it means by 'intent' in what I'm sure is a sincere attempt to stop schools doing what they have done all too often in the past: creating additional work for teachers purely for Ofsted's benefit rather than those they teach. According to their handbook, good intent has the following features:

- 'a curriculum that is ambitious for all pupils'
- 'a curriculum that is coherently planned and sequenced'
- 'a curriculum that is successfully adapted, designed and developed for pupils with special educational needs and/or disabilities'
- 'a curriculum that is broad and balanced for all pupils'[22]

Elsewhere in its inspection handbook, Ofsted does actually attempt to connect a school's curriculum with the real world when they repeat this

---

22. www.bit.ly/33KY44O, accessed 17th December 2019.

statement in both their 'outstanding' and 'good' grade descriptors for the quality of education: 'The school's curriculum is coherently planned and sequenced towards cumulatively sufficient knowledge and skills for future learning and employment.' What I see when I read that, as a consultant who has had to deal with the labyrinthine bureaucracy of EU contracts, is a number of flashing red lights. They place considerable weight on the sequence and accumulation of knowledge, but since inspectors are human beings, and ex-headteachers, they will also expect to see a lot of evidence of planning. Providing that evidence will be time consuming and is almost certainly going to eat into time better spent teaching. When I read it as an ex-English teacher and author, I see a very different-coloured warning light. Ofsted have nothing to offer when it comes to advice about that 'future learning' or 'employment'. That's precisely the point at which *Teaching English for the Real World* matters, because if what you do aligns your curriculum with Ofsted's expectations, yet not with the real world, then is it really worth doing?

In one respect, we should be grateful Ofsted stop short of going there because those that do tend to be the technocrats and 'jobs-that-haven't-been-invented-yet' snake oil salesmen, forging a path for their tech start-up or their personal ambition, regardless of the real nature of learning or jobs. Schools have been the favourite playground for all kinds of people keen to take their untrained social conscience or personal politics for a walk for far too long. The more teachers reject those kinds of pressures and insist on being left alone to teach children, the better for everyone. The children learn more and teachers' working lives improve when they don't feel the burden of repairing every crack in the social fabric some celebrity or politician wants to dump on the school lawn.

There is one final, near-ubiquitous feature of future employment that demands English teachers rethink what they are doing: the presentation. Driven again by new technology, the requirement for employees in all manner of workplaces to stand in front of an audience and present information in a clear and persuasive manner is almost as common as the need for discursive meetings. Not only does the technology urge us to make use of it as a creative tool, it also encourages us to cover far more ground by sharing. Almost every real-time speaking event I attend these days will have some video or software means to capture the various speakers' presentations and redistribute them to a much larger audience afterwards.

English teachers do, of course, ask children to present ideas and information in a classroom setting, and often with the aid of exactly the same software professional adults are using. It's an inefficient activity in terms of the opportunity cost because when one child in 30 is presenting, inevitably, 29 risk just being passive observers unless you have designed a meaningful activity for them simultaneously. Added to this problem is the likelihood that in an English teacher's classroom, the presentation itself will be focused more on the material – on demonstrating that some specific information, usually about books, has been researched or captured – than on the skill of presenting itself. Again, I would ask: which is more important to the child? That they read *Of Mice and Men* and rerun information about Lennie or Steinbeck's technique better dealt with by direct instruction or in lesson conversations, or that they learn how to speak lucidly, persuasively and confidently to an audience? If it's the latter, why are they only addressing their peers? And if they are only addressing their peers, how much more important is it to make sure what they talk about has a degree of authenticity? Why aren't they, as in my earlier example of letter writing, given something to do which is much closer to the reality, so that they appreciate why it's worth their investing time and thought into putting words together on a series of slides or on paper notes they hold in their hand? Is a classroom audience of peers a sufficiently credible proxy for the audience of strangers that many will face time after time beyond the school gates? Because yet again, what you realise when you start to think about teaching English for the real world is that even when the technology thrusts something else at you, in this case graphic design and images, words will always outweigh them.

It's a commonplace in the business world to be advised to include powerful imagery in a slideshow because pictures are more powerful than words. No one's heart skips a beat when a slide pops up decorated with nothing but Times New Roman, and if the presenter then starts to actually read the words on the slide aloud, my heart literally shrivels. I'm astonished how often that actually happens, particularly when people working in education do it. It's one thing to display key text and ask your audience to read and consider it for a moment. Quite another to read it aloud for them. Similarly, when someone says, 'I hope you can read that; it's a bit small,' I have to stifle the urge to shout out, 'And whose fault is that!' I have the same reaction when I see slideshows packed with images and coloured arrows or that look like something cut and pasted from a child's scrapbook. This may sound mean, but people are being paid to do this stuff and they should know better because skilful, successful presentation is far more complex than a choice between words or pictures. To illustrate just how complex, I'm going to run through a number of real-world examples.

Long before the current interest in educational research, I was just one in a large audience watching the director of research at a lavishly funded quango deliver a keynote presentation about educational technology in schools. At one point, she produced a perfectly readable graph, but as she talked over it, it quickly became clear that what she was saying directly contradicted the information on the graph. It wasn't just loosely linked: it was the direct opposite. I wasn't the only one to notice this. A hand went up and another member of the audience politely pointed this out. The presenter's response was to look at the slide for a moment, turn back to the audience member and agree, adding, 'I don't know how that happened,' before merrily continuing: as though nothing had happened. But something really important *had* indeed happened. She had lost most of her audience because no one seriously listening or genuinely 'paying attention' was going to believe anything that followed in those slides, however slick the animation, convincing the statistics or potent the image because her *words* told a very different story.

Much more recently, I watched two academic researchers present their statistical analyses of the London Challenge, a UK government-led initiative widely accredited with transforming London's poorly performing secondary schools between 2003 and 2011 at a total cost of £80 million. Both were excellent speakers and presented the information clearly using visible graphics and clear text. One had concluded the challenge had been reasonably effective; the other argued that it had made no discernible difference at all and any improvements in exam results could be accounted for by demographic factors. A third presentation was given by the ex-civil servant who had led the Challenge, and he too used a combination of different statistics, graphically presented, and text to support the view that it was a roaring success. It was a salutary lesson for every new research school and anyone eager to use research to improve school or teacher performance.

I actually knew what the aims of the London Challenge were; they are publicly available from the King's Fund, who carried out a major case study on it.[23] The Challenge had only three measurable objectives:

- to reduce the number of underperforming schools, especially in relation to English and maths
- to increase the number of schools rated as 'good' or 'outstanding' by Ofsted
- to improve educational outcomes for disadvantaged children

This kind of precision is, in my experience, far more common in business than in education. When money is at stake, people tend to define their team goals more clearly and it's a much healthier place to be when you know you're expected to deliver something so easily measurable, even if it's in an uncertain competition with others, than being a teacher who is somehow meant to be 'accountable' for their pupils' personal performance. So, when it came to questions, given that no one there had been able to convince me or the rest of the audience either way, I asked the ex-civil servant the obvious question. These were your three objectives; can you tell us if you met them? He couldn't and in fact said that they had changed their objectives. I will leave you to decide what that story reveals about educational policy and reform, as well as the importance of presentations.

When the stakes are especially high, businesses are willing to invest more in their effort to win. On one project I worked on, which required a major effort in terms of stakeholder engagement, the team spent two days in a hotel rehearsing. We had a dedicated bid team but it was also considered important that we present to an expected audience of around a thousand, in partnership with our public sector partner. Our hugely experienced sales director exerted every diplomatic bone in his body to encourage the ex-headteacher from the partner to rehearse with us. She dutifully stood in but blithely dismissed any suggestion from him that she might want to write down what she would say. In contrast, I had written and memorised every word I was going to say and had even printed it all onto a little sheaf of small cards I could discreetly refer to in my hand if

---

23. www.bit.ly/2Jf1m78, accessed 19th December 2019.

necessary. When the big day came and it was time for the ex-headteacher to speak, she visibly and spectacularly dried like a toddler with stage fright. I had to step in *and* make it look like I hadn't.

It's not just in the high-stakes commercial context that presentations carry such weight. In all kinds of academic and research contexts, presenting information to an audience can be central to individual or organisational success. If, as Ofsted hope, schools are providing pupils with 'sufficient knowledge and skills for future learning and employment', then teaching them the part presentations play in that world must be a school's responsibility. It's a particularly interesting challenge because when you look at it from a real-world perspective, it raises the interesting question of where in the curriculum it belongs. Can an art department's knowledge about graphics and design be deployed to complement an English department's knowledge? Or do teachers of English need to extend their own knowledge to embrace the use of images and design?

I'm going to try to answer those questions again from real-world experience. At one extreme, I have worked with colleagues who believe a slideshow should be made up entirely of persuasive statistics and images. They have no time for a well-crafted sentence or even phrase. They inevitably work in technology. Others have been less restrictive and appreciate the power of a clear and memorable message that relies entirely on the right words in the right order and maybe a bit of colour. Wise companies design a set of standard, branded templates for employees to use, which stops them wasting time or having to fret over design choices. Few don't grasp that it's far too easy to overload the audience's episodic memory and almost everyone understands the power of repetition. There are even professionals whose job is to teach others how to present. One of my employers provided training in what they called 'high-impact presentation' for business development staff, and I attended one of those courses not long after leaving the classroom. It was fascinating because it brought home to me just how transferable teaching skills are. Having spent almost 20 years standing up in front of a classroom audience for hours every day, I thought nothing of doing so in front of a tiny group of colleagues in this course; but for others, it was a nightmare. A friend who held such a senior role in his particular industry that he was often asked to speak at international conferences about it once confided in me that he dreaded the entire experience so much, he always broke out in cold sweat beforehand, no matter how well he'd prepared or rehearsed. On my course, it became visibly clear to me that this activity I regarded as routine was a considerable challenge to others. The professional trainer ended up using me repeatedly as a model because so much of what he was teaching I had learned already, merely by being a teacher. Where you stand in a room, the tone and stress patterning of your voice, how you use your eyes to engage everyone in front of you, how you move about and emphasise those things you want your audience to walk away with, how you read your audience's reaction and level of understanding – these were all walked through in detail during this course. They are bread and butter to a skilled teacher, so my answer to that question about where teaching about presenting belongs in a secondary school curriculum? I think it rests firmly on the English department's plate.

My 'high-impact presentations' course taught me some valuable ideas about structuring presentations, which I still use. I always begin by justifying my presence as best I can. I tell people why I'm there and what qualifies me to talk about the subject. I list what I'm going to cover and keep people aware of where I am in the list as I progress. Even if I'm speaking for an hour, I try not to cover too much information and make sure I repeat less than a handful of key ideas I want to embed in my audience's semantic memory. If people don't walk out remembering those few things, then my impact has been negligible.

Years of doing this kind of work has also taught me something I could never have learned on a course. However large the audience, or physical space, I try to scan every face I can in order to capture people's attention and to monitor their reaction to me. Impossible, of course, when your audience is 900 strong and so far away you can't read any kind of facial response. But those large audiences are the exception, and experience has convinced me that no matter what I'm talking about, however skilfully I've worded things or however fascinating the slides, someone is going to hate me. At least one person, quite possibly more, will not react as I would like them to. So, I have devised a personal metric for my success that's about how many people want to speak to me afterwards. The more who feel able to approach me either immediately after the presentation's over, or later on the same day, the more successful I feel I've been. None of this is exclusive – I've no doubt other people have other strategies – but it is real.

CHAPTER TWO
UNDOING THE TYRANNY OF GCSE

GCSE and the curriculum

Having outlined the real-world context in which schools are operating, in this second chapter I'll focus on what should be happening in the early years of secondary schooling to reflect that context, before the tyranny of GCSE (or any other national assessment exam) kicks in and everything happening in the English classroom becomes about every child's performance in one or two exams. Before that, it's worth taking time to understand the history here and the various pressures at play. The GCSE has always been thought of as a two-year course. Exam boards align their syllabuses with English national curriculum requirements for key stage 4, which is legally the two-year period of education most 15- and 16-year-olds will undertake and which is expected will embrace a programme of study covering a range of subjects. This range of subjects varies a little within the UK but it always includes English. Pertinently, Scotland, and now Wales, have in recent years made major curriculum changes to reflect what they believe the real world looks like. They refer more to literacy and talk more about skills for life and work, but the real driver for both nations' desire for change has been, unsurprisingly, technology. I worked regularly in Scotland on a national educational technology programme which coincided with the inception of their Curriculum for Excellence and saw first-hand this influence at play. While Scotland is much further down the road and its political leaders now find themselves facing increasing criticism for poor PISA performance and a growing sense amongst educators and parents that standards are indeed slipping, Wales is currently in the throes of hurling themselves down the same primrose path to transience. New Zealand seems hell-bent on the same politicised trajectory. The Welsh interest in technology is reflected in a new 'digital competence framework' designed to introduce digital skills across the curriculum and prepare children for 'the opportunities and risks that an online world presents'. Given everything I've been saying up until this point, I should be a fan, but I'm not.

There are powerful cultural, political and commercial influences at play in both nations, very different from any in England. Look closely at Scotland's Curriculum for Excellence, for example, and you will find politicians' inky fingerprints all over it. Two of its four capacities, 'responsible citizens' and 'effective contributors', are unashamedly utilitarian in purpose. This is state education for the state, not the individual. Both the Welsh and Scottish curriculums also exhibit an interest in health and well-being that speaks more of recent political preoccupations than of the fundamental educational needs of teenagers. Ever since Tony Blair traduced the word three times for entirely political ends, education has become every campaigning individual's go-to tool. The teaching profession has allowed itself to become deeply politicised from within, and one of the most damaging side effects has been an exponential growth in responsibility. Schools are easy pickings for lobbyists eager to change things. By allowing themselves to be portrayed as altruists above all else, teachers lost sight of what it means to be a *teaching* professional and schools became vulnerable to every lobbyist, campaigner and celebrity with a pet cause to espouse.

I worked as a tutor for Teach First in their inaugural summer school and have been a supporter of the organisation ever since, because whatever else you may think of them, they have put many hundreds of excellent young teachers into schools who might well have gone elsewhere. But one thing I have always felt they got dangerously wrong was the messaging they used to recruit. Instead of stressing subject specialism and scholarship, they focused entirely on 'making a difference', on convincing idealistic young men and women they could 'change lives'. When writing this, I took a look at their current website, and if you watch the video there you will see that exact phrase, 'making a difference', makes an appearance in less than 20 seconds.[24] Substitute the odd word here or there, and the entire video could quite easily be aimed at social workers, nurses, or the police. There is no sense of what

---

24. www.teachfirst.org.uk, accessed 4th January 2020.

it means to be a scholarly teaching professional, passionate about your subject and skilled at conveying knowledge to others. Recruits in those first few years were repeatedly told they would be the people who shaped future society. Ironically, it was an object lesson in real-world English. If you employ an international management consultancy to design a national teacher recruitment programme, don't be surprised if they craft some skilful messages. Or, as lots of chief executives know only too well, when they show no interest whatsoever in the long-term impact the moment they've banked the cheque. The same kind of appealing rhetoric is now being used by national governments, keen to address a recruitment crisis created by political incompetence. Quite something when you think about it.

Historically, both Scotland and Wales see themselves as junior partners in the UK, a cultural sensitivity that the Scottish National Party has brilliantly exploited. It remains one of the most baffling features of contemporary British politics that a party with such flagrantly nationalist passions and hatreds has managed to distance itself so effectively from its foreign (and particularly its English) cousins. You can change the colour of the shirt but a nationalist is a nationalist the world over. This junior partner status makes both nations more susceptible to the seductive innovation message commercial technology always promises. There is a clear desire not to be left behind and risk being seen as predominantly rural economies. Ironically, nationalist politicians love nothing more than performing on an international stage. This desire finds its way into the curriculum, which becomes a vehicle for delivering a brave new world. The language of the Curriculum for Excellence resounds with this ambition. That trademark phrase of techno zealotry, the '21st century', is there, as is the belief that this curriculum will help children 'flourish in today's world'. One of six curriculum entitlements, 'a broad general education', has this entirely political ambition added on: 'This includes understanding the world, Scotland's place in it and the environment, referred to as Learning for Sustainability.' Would anyone with a disciplined and professional focus on the educational needs of teenagers have decided to make sure what they are taught included Scotland's place in the world, or that learning must now have an overarching environmental purpose?

Mimicking Scotland's 'four capacities', the proposed curriculum for Wales offers these four curriculum purposes:

- **Ambitious, capable learners** who are ready to learn throughout their lives
- **Enterprising, creative contributors** who are ready to play a full part in life and work
- **Ethical, informed citizens** who are ready to be citizens of Wales and the world
- **Healthy, confident individuals** who are ready to lead fulfilling lives as valued members of society

Wales's international ambitions appear in this additional statement: 'There will be both a "Welsh dimension" and an "international perspective" to the Curriculum for Wales.'[25] The glaring similarity with Scotland's four capacities – 'successful learners', 'confident individuals', 'responsible citizens' and 'effective contributors' – isn't surprising given that the same educational figure, Professor Graham Donaldson, is responsible for both.

It's a truly depressing reflection of the consequences of handing the reins of educational policy over to politicians that while both nations recognised that the world has indeed moved on and left schools and teachers behind, neither understood the nature of that new world or took the time to work out what it was they were trying to prepare children for. (The flightiest racehorse will gallop like the crow flies if you put the kind of blinkers on it most party politicians wear every day they go to work.) The closest anyone got was the Welsh designation of '*digital competence*', along with 'literacy' and 'numeracy', as one of three 'cross-curricular responsibilities' to be taught across all six 'Areas of Learning and Experience':

- Expressive arts
- Health and well-being
- Humanities
- Languages, literacy and communication
- Mathematics and numeracy
- Science and technology

---

25. www.bit.ly/3alqyot, accessed January 3rd 2019.

Yet in spite of its undoubted commitment to detail, the Welsh digital competence framework reads more like a cross between Microsoft 101 and charitable advice about teenage online behaviour than a distinct body of knowledge suited to the real world of employment and social interaction online. Children studying under the new Welsh curriculum will work through five 'progression stages' between the ages of 5 and 16. Wales has taken an unusual position on assessment which is so distinctive I've captured it below in figure 3:

Assessment and progression

The new curriculum will primarily use assessment for the purpose of **informing teaching and learning, rather than accountability** which the Welsh Government has emphasised is covered by other means – primarily the school categorisation system and Estyn inspections. Assessment will therefore predominantly be **formative** (used for on-going pupil development purposes) rather than summative (measuring the progress of a pupil at the end of a defined period of time for benchmarking purposes).

The new Curriculum for Wales will apply from the age of 3 to 16 and provide for a **continuum of learning** rather than the separation of schooling into key stages as at present. The new curriculum will therefore measure learners' progress through expected **'Achievement Outcomes'** at five **'Progression Steps'** at ages 5, 8, 11, 14 and 16. These Achievement Outcomes are written in the form of 'I can', 'I have' etc.

Figure 3 From the *In Brief* report by Senedd Research for the National Assembly of Wales, 'The Draft Curriculum for Wales 2022'.

When you locate the draft of the digital competence framework, you find a long list of model assessment statements for each progression stage that begin, 'Learners are able to...'. Here are just two examples of what pupils are expected to be able to do aged 16: 'understand the ways websites and companies collect data online and utilise it to personalise content for their users, e.g. personal data being shared' and 'explain the ethical issues of corporate encryption, e.g. building in a bypass system'. I'd hate to be the one who has to estimate the CPD costs of realistically getting Welsh teachers to the point where they are able to teach either of those successfully. In the draft spreadsheet, there are 13 different 'elements' accompanying five different topics, often with five or six of these

'Learners are able to…' statements so that, aged 16, you might well be looking at 65 things to assess under the digital competency framework alone. There is a profound educational implication here that the Curriculum for Excellence also failed to understand, in spite of the considerable energy it expended on trying to explain to teachers how they would assess this new curriculum. The moment you think that 'Learners are able to…' or 'I can…' statements should be used as assessment tools, you have shifted the focus of lessons wholesale from knowledge to skills. The English language does that for you. The instruction teachers hear is one that emphasises action over knowledge, physical activity over cerebral. To be fair, the Curriculum for Excellence acknowledges the shift because if you study its assessment advice, you will find numerous references to 'skills'. It repeatedly mentions 'high-order skills' and 'developing skills'. It even talks about the necessity of children 'developing their skills in self and peer assessment and in recognising and evaluating evidence of their own learning'.[26] One paragraph in particular exposes the dangers implicit in moving assessment away from knowledge to skills:

> Assessment should support children and young people in developing the four capacities and the characteristics associated with them. These include a range of personal qualities and skills that in the past may not always have been formally assessed, such as thinking creatively and independently, working in partnership and in teams, making informed decisions and evaluating environmental, scientific and technological issues. These skills and attributes are embedded in the experiences and outcomes. Assessment needs to focus on these, as well as on measuring factual recall and routine procedures.[27]

'Factual recall and routine procedures' is a technocrat's euphemism for knowledge. It's abundantly clear from this key paragraph that what children *know* is regarded as far less important than what they can *show*. It's worth really interrogating this aspect of the Curriculum for Excellence because it's the source both of professional teachers' doubts and criticism

---

26. www.bit.ly/2WKiObG, accessed 8th January 2020.
27. www.bit.ly/3aae2Hm, accessed 8th January 2020.

and of less trustworthy assessment outcomes than conventional summative examinations. Those 'personal qualities and skills that in the past
may not always have been formally assessed' all sound very real-world,
as though someone thought about what happens in employment and
further education and made a serious effort to reflect a future need. But
in the real world, most people are, if you simply think in terms of numbers, not genuinely creative. To be creative means to be able to produce
something others can't. It singles you out in every walk of life. Similarly,
not everyone is good at working in partnership or in teams, nor are they
necessarily going to be even interested in – never mind be able to evaluate – environmental, scientific and technological issues. The only skill I
would agree is both widely necessary and valuable is making informed
decisions. It is all of these things because it has a vital part to play in every
individual's employment, cultural and social life. It matters because any
adult whose education has not enabled them to make informed decisions
is not a free citizen because freedom is choice. The more one scrutinises
the Curriculum for Excellence, the more one sees the blinkered political
mindset reflected in its focus on state, not individual, prosperity.

The essential point I want to emphasise by this digression into Welsh
and Scottish curriculum reform is that it's one thing to recognise there's
a gap between what schools teach and the real world, quite another to
effectively bridge it.

The foundations

Before taking a detailed look at GCSE in England, I want to concentrate
on the first few years of secondary school English teaching and explore
what should be done in those crucial, foundational years, to better reflect
the real world of English I described in chapter one. What could schools
be doing differently that would lay the foundations for children to leave,
ensuring they had the English skills and knowledge to cope with what
really lay in store for them in employment, higher education and society?

The first thing I would want to see is a substantial series of lessons on
basic linguistics and etymology. English has come to occupy a unique role
in the world. It's much of the world's mother tongue, half the world's second
language and the universal language of diplomacy, research and business.
Perhaps most surprisingly, even the EU admits that 'English dominates as

the language that Europeans are most likely to be able to speak'. It is easily the most widely spoken foreign language at 38%, while French stands at only 12%, German 11%, Spanish 7% and Russian a mere 5%.[28]

Schools should be providing everyone they teach with background knowledge that tells them where English came from, what kind of language it is, and the major historical events that led to its current status. This means introducing and thoroughly embedding linguistic concepts like inflection, syntax and phonology. It also means abandoning completely any notion of children experimenting with language, the naive anarchy of so much post-'60s English teaching, before they know how it works. This *Through the Looking-Glass* English teaching reached its zenith for me when I was still teaching and attending a training session run by a GCSE exam board. The examiner running the session showed a number of examples of children's work, which was largely unintelligible due to poor handwriting and incorrect spelling. Nonetheless, she spent the session explaining how to award marks by guessing what the writer intended. It still has a worrying grip on many corners of the profession and vocal advocates outside the classroom are given far too much air time by the mainstream media to peddle this kind of deeply damaging, naive ideology.

These early lessons should cover the existence of Celtic languages spoken by native inhabitants of these islands, as well as the Latin of the period of Roman occupation before connecting English clearly to the Anglo-Saxon settlers who brought it with them from Denmark and other parts of mainland Europe in the fifth to seventh centuries. Children should be introduced to the Old English of *Beowulf* used by the Anglo-Saxons, told about the Norman invasion and how Anglo-Norman morphed into something historians now call Middle English before lessons on the Early Modern English of Shakespeare and finally the Modern English of Dr Johnson and Henry Fielding we have largely inherited today. Imagine teaching the kinds of texts that currently dominate GCSE English Literature to a class that had this kind of linguistic and historical schema in their heads to refer to. Imagine them just confidently knowing how closely connected English is to Latin, German and French and why. This is learning, not cultural capital.

---

28. EU Commission, (2012), *Europeans and Their Languages,* Report, p. 19.

Alongside these lessons, pupils need specific teaching about orthography to get them (as quickly as possible in the first two years of secondary school) to the point where they can use their knowledge of English to express their understanding of other curriculum subjects. Comprehending the difference between a grapheme and a phoneme; knowing the most common uses of all the key punctuation marks; but most significantly, understanding the importance of orthography as a professional and personal discipline – these should be the cornerstones of good English teaching in these early years. It's precisely when these key elements of effective language use are either only partially taught or imperfectly grasped that scores of children in secondary schools start experiencing that dreadful euphemism for not teaching them the right things: intervention.

I'm aware that some English teachers may be thinking, 'But we do that already; we just don't call it that.' Which I think is part of the problem. I suspect where it is done, it's more as a complement to, or diversion from, the kind of core reading and creative writing lessons I referred to in chapter one, when it should be overshadowing and underpinning them. Children in these early secondary school years need to understand why things are being taught in the sequence that they are. The damage caused by telling young children to think of language like plasticine, something colourful and malleable but entirely at their mercy, can't be underestimated. It resonates through adult life and is the precursor, amongst other things, to an entire world of excruciatingly ill-disciplined poetry. If children were taught to think about musical notation in the same way, every journey in a hotel lift would be taken in a fog of cacophonous sound; every wait on a phone, a misery of metallic dissonance.

Poetry provides the best example of the damage because it has been so doubtfully taught in schools for so long. The world is full of successful, educated, book-buying metrophobes who walk past the poetry shelf in Waterstones as though it were labelled 'Body Odour: Self Help'. Almost all the energy and focus is placed on personal expression ('pupil voice', if you like), with none of the detailed linguistic understanding about sound and meaning, rhythm and convention that is required to produce linguistically disciplined, aesthetically credible poetry, worthy of its ancestry. This weakness goes right to the top of the poetic tree. Speaking on the BBC's Radio 4 *Today* programme on national poetry day in 2019, the poet Nikita

Gill dropped this trite bombshell: 'All poetry is political. Even poems about flowers are political,' while the poet laureate Simon Armitage and the BBC's Mishal Husain invisibly nodded. Listen, as I do, to a lot of poetry, and one of the most dispiriting experiences is how often you hear a published poet effectively sabotage their own work by performing it in a pompous, self-consciously 'poetic' monotone, as though poetry had no relationship with sound whatsoever. This is what happens when you buy into the narcissistic lie that the personal is political. All that matters is that *you* express *your*self. Stick to your guns, keep telling yourself you're a poet and people will eventually come to believe it, even if when you read your verse aloud it sounds like you wrote it on a blackboard with your fingernails.

Effective self-expression is an entirely appropriate goal for teachers aiming to teach children how to make those 'informed decisions' favoured by the Curriculum for Excellence, but when it's taught as an idealistic, creative end in itself, as it so often is in poetry and other creative writing lessons, it crumbles in the rubble of its own weak foundations.

Children should appreciate that what they are taught in these early years about orthography and linguistics will inform how they write and, crucially, think throughout their school career and beyond. If the absence of such teaching merely generated a lot of weak, self-indulgent poetry published in literary magazines with names like *Ink, Sweat and Beers* or *Verbosium* with a circulation in the hundreds, it might not matter so much; but it has a much wider, pernicious impact on thought itself, which anyone familiar with how the language is used on social media will be acutely aware of. Discussion and debate rely on a mutually respectful exchange of language that becomes impossible where the rules haven't been learnt. The more basic the linguistic tools you have at hand, the narrower your scope for thought (a limitation that has no respect for job titles or, indeed, presidential mandates). Stray into the world of contemporary politics in any medium you care to mention, and you will quickly see the problems caused when individuals only have access to bargain basement linguistic tools.

Supporting all this early work on linguistics and etymology, secondary schools should also commit to teaching children in these first two years how to write clearly, by hand. At the risk of upsetting a chunk of readers, it has to be said, I've seen handwriting by US senior executives that would embarrass an eight-year-old. This happens because of an early overreliance on keyboards. The pressure on secondary schools to move to online exams is entirely driven by technology businesses who turn a blind eye to any ethical discussion about how such a radical shift might impact on children's ability to think coherently or independently. English teachers abdicating their responsibility to ensure pupils can write fluently by hand is akin to maths teachers thinking kids can get by without immediate recall of multiplication tables. You are undermining the very foundations of learning. Look at the marketing of technologies in education over the past few decades and the sales pitch is almost always drawn from a very short menu. Technology is nearly always 'innovative', it saves busy people time and is more efficient. In the case of online assessment, there is the additional promise of greater accuracy as well as speed, although the track record of some of the major players has been unimpressive.[29] Personally, I've always thought the marketing people miss a trick here. Every experienced teacher will recognise that conversation with a child that begins, 'But Miss X doesn't like me, sir.' Assessment software offers them neutrality as well as accuracy. None of these advantages counters the risks that come with ill thought through uses of technology in education. I'm saving the full discussion for the last chapter of the book, but here is one prime example of why it's important to make a decision to embed good handwriting skills early in the secondary English teaching classroom. Susan M. Dynarski, in an article for the Brookings Institution[30] ('Online schooling: who is harmed and who is helped?'), cites a number of research projects in US colleges and high schools that examine the impact of online learning by asking the key question, 'Are online courses fulfilling their promise?' She concludes that 'a clear pattern emerges: academically challenged students do worse in online than in face-to-face courses'. There is good reason why handwriting is often a quick and dirty indicator for teachers of a child's ability in English: it is the de facto means by which they communicate their thought and knowledge. Moving a child who is struggling with handwriting to a learning

29. Pearson, the world's largest education business has had a troubled history delivering online testing; and Fair Test, The National Center for Fair & Open Testing in the US, reported that 42 states had had at least one widespread disruption of test administration due to technology failure between 2013 and 2019.

30. www.brook.gs/2R4NZef, accessed 9th January 2020.

environment in which human biomechanics are replaced by a keyboard (and all the complex variety of additional aids to writing that come with it) is likely to have two major downsides. It may mask weaknesses such as spelling and punctuation; and it may embed the idea that words are located externally, not generated cerebrally, before the child has either a breadth of vocabulary or facility with semantics to express themselves sufficiently well to access the rest of the school curriculum. What else are predictive text and emojis but invitations not to think?

I suspect many secondary school English teachers will still think teaching a child handwriting falls outside their professional remit. Yet in the real world, many children start secondary school still struggling with basics the system hoped to embed by the time they leave primary education. This applies equally to reading. Secondary schools are generally better at accepting the challenge to address the latter than the particularly onerous task of improving a child's handwriting. Organisations like the National Handwriting Association can help English teachers decide how best to teach these children without having to reinvent the wheel, as though the mere fact that a child has changed schools requires a different approach. It's not at all unlikely that in any single classroom in the first year of secondary school, there will be children whose cursive handwriting is secure and even graceful sitting alongside others who still battle with the motor skills necessary to write legibly. The longer the latter struggle, the wider the gap will get, and the dominant whole-class teaching model of the secondary curriculum doesn't help. But interventions and additional support are time consuming, expensive, often delivered by people without the right skills and can come with a curriculum opportunity cost for the individual child, which is far too easily overlooked. As a secondary school English teacher, being knowledgeable (as well as able to simply advise a child in a class full of them) about the mechanics of their handwriting is a much more economic and educationally valid process than frequently taking children out of the same lesson for an hour with a teaching assistant.

In chapter one, I discussed writing and why it's so important to think carefully about the reasons you give children to write and to design activities that make it easier for them to think, because writing simply doesn't happen without thought. This was neatly illustrated for me when, as I was writing this section, an English teacher in my Twitter network tweeted this simple plea: 'Is it just me or does anyone else hate modelling writing? I can't think on the spot.' This cuts right to the heart of what English teachers need to consider when designing authentic writing tasks for children in these early secondary years. When we ask them to copy examples of conventional devices like simile and metaphor, or to write descriptively from an image, or give them an example of vivid prose to mimic, we aren't really teaching them *how* to write but *what* to write. The difference is a profound one. I'm not suggesting these tasks aren't without some value, but their value is minimal compared to tasks which effectively provoke children to think before they write down their thoughts. I used diary writing as an example of authentic writing in chapter one and repeat that I can think of no better way of starting secondary English classes than to be gifted an attractive, formal diary that you are told is your personal property for life. The concept of a diary is not difficult to teach, but I would question the value of taking the obvious next step and bolstering that information with examples from famous historical diarists. Whether you opt for someone obvious like Samuel Pepys or Virginia Woolf, or find something more contemporary from Alan Bennett, or something unusual like Bruce Frederick Cummings's *The Journal of a Disappointed Man*, you risk undermining the vital thing you've provided: an opportunity to establish thinking for themselves as a habit.

There is of course nothing to stop you looking at diary writing as a genre at a later date (work that would obviously be more successful with habitual diarists), but personal accounts are not restricted to diarists and they also provide one of the best routes into nonfiction reading for children.

As I explained in chapter one, diary writing is an effective tool because it gives pupils a reason to think, and that signals a way to start thinking in turn as an English teacher about other, more effective ways to get children writing. Lesson time spent stimulating and encouraging thought – for example by nurturing a whole-class discussion steered and managed by you on any topic your knowledge of them suggests might captivate them – should provide a much firmer platform from which they can subsequently write. The trick, it seems to me, is simply not to prepare or announce a written task until you have effectively provoked them to genuinely *think* about something – an instruction all too easy to deliver but way more difficult to guarantee or even observe. This might not be as daunting as it first sounds if you consider how common it is for English teachers to know exactly how to provoke their pupils.

I think it's easy to fall into a conventional trap here and opt for group discussion as a strategy. English classrooms are full of children sitting in small groups being given instructions to look at some information or written material and then 'discuss' it. The quickest and most intellectually agile won't have much difficulty, but is that true of the majority? Thought is quintessentially personal, private and demanding. It is hard work for a young teenager to assimilate then reflect on someone else's words or ideas before articulating a genuinely personal response. They face all kinds of social and developmental barriers to this kind of demand.

Anyone familiar with educational research and pedagogical debate will know that many experienced teachers choose the word 'craft' to describe what they do. If you imagine for a moment standing in front of a class and devoting 15 or 20 minutes of a lesson just to provoking them to think about something, I suspect you'll quickly appreciate that all kinds of pedagogical skills come into play, difficult to define or list. You are likely to choose your own words spontaneously but nonetheless carefully, use a rich variety of shifts in tone of voice and facial expression. You may well use humour or anecdote. You will monitor every child's reactions in the room as you speak, simultaneously managing their responses, interventions and reactions to each other, so that the conversation progresses civilly and productively. What you might not be doing is continually asking yourself: are they all really *thinking* about this? If the answer to that question is 'yes', then when the time comes for you to introduce the written task, the chances of lucid sentences quickly forming on everyone's blank pages are going to be substantially increased, compared to if you simply outlined a written task for them, showed them some examples and then told them to start writing. How common is it, when you have issued that conventional written task, to spend the next ten minutes of a lesson answering questions from pupils who haven't begun to write yet because what is really happening is that they are using you to do the thinking for them?

There is a whole vipers' nest of pedagogy that believes learning should be stimulating but which reduces stimulation to a three-letter word: fun. Children at this age will obviously choose a chance to play if offered one instead of hard work, but the funsters make the same mistake as those who think books need to be relevant. They abdicate their role as teacher in favour of something much easier. Great teachers do indeed stimulate children, but to think, not play. If you distilled all those millions of memories most adults have of inspirational teachers, my bet is most would agree with one simple statement: 'They made me think.'

From writing, I want to turn to arguably a greater challenge for real-world children at this age: reading. At the FutureBook Live Conference in London, organised by *The Bookseller* magazine in 2019, the CEO of Waterstones, James Daunt, delivered a keynote on the future of bookselling. One audience member asked him about teenagers' reading habits. 'Are you worried,' she said, 'that teenagers' screen lives are preventing them from becoming readers?' His answer was dismissive and blunt: 'No,' based, he said, on Waterstones's healthy young adult fiction sales figures. I couldn't help wondering how an audience full of English teachers, not publishers and authors, might have reacted. In their latest annual report, *Children and Young People's Reading*, the National Literacy Trust say that 'levels of daily reading decreased for a second consecutive year, falling from 32% in 2016 to 30.8% in 2017/18'.[31]

The technological issues related to reading that the questioner raised will have to wait until the final chapter. Here, I want to think about reading, as I've done about writing. Given the real-world situation I've described in chapter one, what needs to be done about reading in these early years in secondary school? What should children be reading in these first few years? How should we approach the whole business? Doug Lemov and his US colleagues have dedicated a lot of thought to this and to devising a wide range of practical strategies to nurture successful high-school readers.[32] I don't intend to replay or challenge their work. What I want to do here is maintain this book's focus on the real world and start not by worrying over why some children are still struggling to read in their early teens and what can be done about it, but by asking the question (given what they will be faced with as adults): what should mainstream English teachers do to consolidate reading as a routine skill in those first few years, before the tyranny of GCSE sets in? Not coincidentally, I think, while researching, I came across a school that has

---

31. www.bit.ly/2WMMjcU, accessed, 17th January 2020.

32. See Lemov, Doug, Driggs Colleen and Woolway, Erica., (2016). *Reading Reconsidered*, Jossey Bass.

a specific strategy to use what they call 'real-world articles' to nurture nonfiction reading skills.

A core goal of every secondary school English department must be to get children to the point where they are comfortable, confident, regular readers of books as soon as possible after they start their secondary education. A fortunate minority will be there already, but it is a common mistake to assume that a child is a confident and habitual reader because they can read fluently aloud in a classroom. The world is full of children who sail through summative exams like GCSEs in the UK, even English literature exams, but who leave school two years later with neither a habit nor a love of reading. Any teacher who thinks a child can't gain a top grade in GCSE English Literature without reading any of the set texts isn't concentrating. Why do children themselves think they can get away with this? What happens that allows them to feel emboldened enough to sit for 90 minutes in an examination hall, answering questions about texts they have never read, without even sweating?

One key reason is the extreme lengths teachers go to to support them instead of teaching them. Online conversations between English teachers and online repositories are full of shared lesson resources and material aimed at doing just this. Educationally, teachers start from the wrong assumption. They are frequently told (and convince themselves) that without their support, children will simply not do the reading summative exams demand, and so neglect to inculcate the scholarly habits and attitudes towards learning per se that would render that effort unnecessary. Texts that have been lavishly annotated, skilful model answers, detailed notes and analyses, all written by teachers, not pupils – these all proliferate online and are eagerly consumed as reusable resources by many teachers.

A second major reason is undoubtedly beyond teachers' control. Our wider culture does little to encourage young teenagers to be habitual readers of books, while doing much to nurture their addiction to screens. Schools have been put on the back foot in this fight for children's attention by businesses intent on selling them entertainment. The real-world screen offers endless attractions to adolescent minds, some deeply unsavoury, but apart from taking the obvious step to minimise their use in school time, there is only so much teachers can do to counter this immense, external cultural pressure. The most alluring activities for teenagers – contemporary music, dating and shopping – have moved online en masse in recent years. Reading books, an activity that is solitary, time consuming and solipsistic, is entirely opposed in nature to screen life, which is shared, snatched at every opportunity and transient. In this technologically determined society, the onus for schools to turn all children into habitual and capable readers of hard-copy books falls heaviest on English teachers. I'll save a look at what the research says about screen versus hard-copy reading for the final chapter on technology, but for now I hope you'll agree that all English teachers have a dog in this fight. Unfortunately, it's a Shih Tzu.

Tackling this wider cultural pressure requires English teachers to address the issue head on. It's a case of 'know your enemy'. Instead of seeking technological solutions, online or comic book versions of set texts, teachers should position the issue as a key part of the curriculum. At the same time pupils are learning about the history and significance of English through lessons on etymology and linguistics, arguments about the importance of reading books should be openly discussed, and an unequivocal case made for the habit as a foundation to all future learning and work. It isn't enough to just talk about this generally or leave the librarian to do it. It needs embedding formally in the English curriculum as an explicit goal before children reach the age of 15. Again, without delving too deep into questions for a later section, the stable door to ethical technology has been left open for about 20 years. It rotted and dropped off its hinges before most politicians or academics had noticed, which is why they are now frantically trying to catch up. As I write, the Royal College of Psychiatrists has just got around to demanding social media businesses hand over their vast datasets to academics, so that they can study what sort of content users are viewing. The horse, meanwhile, is in another county.

Today's children face a future where the manual jobs that have supplied work for vast numbers of mostly uneducated adults are fast dwindling away. If there is one thing technology is good at doing, it's man's dirty work. This is as true medically as it is militarily. More and more of those you teach will need the English knowledge and skills you teach if they are to find employment. This doesn't require some overhyped fourth industrial revolution. It just requires evolution, which as we all know is inevitable.

Children need to learn that concentrated silent reading is a fundamental skill for their entire school career, and for the vast majority of professional careers and employment routes they are likely to follow post school. Those who simply can't envisage such a future need to know the personal consequences. We need to explain clearly to them the impact on their personal lives as well as their careers. The adult who is content to read merely what state or commercial bureaucracy requires of them, who settles for a bookless, textless life and relies on the conversation of acquaintances, friends and family to inform them, is free only in the most limited sense. Large numbers of children are simply behind in their reading when they start, and lots of schools invest heavily in time, people and all kinds of additional resources aimed at helping them to catch up.

Faced with her own children who wouldn't read, Judith Hall, from Port Edwards in Wisconsin, created a bit of software that encouraged them to read by setting them multiple-choice tests on the content of classic novels Judith selected for them and ranked by what she personally judged was their difficulty. Today, the idea Judith developed has become Accelerated Reader, one of a range of software products sold by the company Renaissance and used by over 52,000 schools in 82 countries to support pupils in basic reading and maths. It's very popular with English teachers facing the precise challenge I'm describing, not least because it gives them a simple way to match a child's reading age to a book. To do this, it uses something called the Lexile scale, which is a widely used measure of textual difficulty in the US. No teachers I've met have any idea what the Lexile scale is, or know anything about how it goes about calculating a neatly acceptable reading level for any book. This is what it actually does. It looks at a short extract from a book, often as little as 150 or 250 words, before assessing the word difficulty by simply counting the numbers of letters and syllables in the words. It judges sentence complexity by measuring the length in words and/or the number of phrases. It then puts these two figures together to provide a reading age level for the entire book. All the major readability scales calculate in similar ways. That is all they do.

The Lexile scale is an entirely quantitative measure. I'll let that sink in. It has no way of measuring a text's difficulty except by word and sentence length, which of course means it can't measure difficulty at all. It was the result of a series of grants made by the National Institute of Child Health and Human Development in the US through their small business innovation programme, between 1984 and 1996, to the Metametrics business founded by Jackson Stenner and Malbert Smith. Metametrics makes this claim on its website today: 'With the creation of the Lexile Framework for Reading, Jack and Malbert demonstrated that common scales, like Fahrenheit and Celsius, could be built for academic skills.'[33] – a statement that, were it to appear in front of me in an English essay by a student, I would feel bound to circle in red ink and annotate with the phrase, 'Your comparison sucks.'

The idea that any text has a discrete, accurately measurable reading level is itself nonsensical. It's predicated on a crude model of reading as nothing more than decoding. Many teachers are familiar with the baseball study by Recht and Leslie[34] and with subsequent experiments that have always replicated its findings. In simple terms, what their study exposed was how important prior knowledge is to reading comprehension. Faced with a 625-word passage describing a half-inning of a baseball game, low-ability readers with high prior knowledge of baseball outperformed high-ability readers with low prior knowledge of baseball. What this study and later replications all confirm is the vital part prior knowledge, and especially vocabulary, plays in any child's reading comprehension. Labelling a child with a reading age and then encouraging them to read only books that have also been allocated a reading age by means of readability software (which is frequently how schools use a resource like Accelerated Reader) seems unlikely to deliver many educational benefits for the child.

Yet following their own research, the EEF regards Accelerated Reader as one of very few Promising Projects, delivering what they describe as an additional three months' progress in the course of an academic year:

> Accelerated Reader has also been tested through a previous EEF efficacy trial involving four secondary schools and 350 Year 7 pupils. The study randomised pupils within each of the schools and focused particularly on pupils who did not achieve a level 4 on their Key Stage 2 SATs. The project found a positive impact on all pupils of an additional three months' progress over the

---

33. www.bit.ly/39sKAMv, accessed 15th January 2020.
34. Recht, Donna R, and Leslie, Lauren. (1988) 'Effect of Prior Knowledge on Good and Poor Readers' Memory of Text', *Journal of Educational Psychology*, Vol. 80, no. 1, 16-20.

course of an academic year. The results also suggested that AR was particularly beneficial for children eligible for free school meals, with these pupils making an additional five months' progress, however due to the smaller sample size this result was less secure.[35]

Writing in *Psychology Today* in 2017, Paula J. Schwanenflugel and Nancy Flanagan Knapp explored the workings of readability software in an essay entitled 'Three Myths About "Reading Levels" – and why you shouldn't fall for them…'.[36] They point out that running the same text through seven different, popular reading scales produces a range spanning three grade levels. It's an easy experiment to carry out for yourself if you are interested. The Lexile Analyzer is available online[37] and it's quite amusing to see what it makes of D.H. Lawrence, Virginia Woolf or Ian Rankin. I recommend you try it. If you ever had any, your faith in reading levels will never be the same again.

Literacy remains a mountain for some children to climb. Teachers do of course talk a lot about children's futures and the consequences of passing or failing summative exams, but how often does a school's English curriculum clearly explain the personal consequences of practical or near illiteracy? How often is the need to think of quietly, thoughtfully and routinely reading books as the basis for knowing and learning adequately stressed? How far do schools go in weakening that resolve in the face of the wider cultural pressures to use technology or to personalise learning?

I want to turn now to thinking about reading as much from the individual professional teacher's point of view as possible, because it is often the individual, and not a larger team, that makes key decisions about what pupils should read. In his 1644 essay *Of Education*, John Milton, partly in reaction to what he saw as the stultifying effects of medieval education and Catholicism, put his remarkable mind to work on the question of what should be taught and how. Like many people today with less expansive imaginations, Milton saw education primarily as a state business, the best way to manufacture good citizens. But there is one idea

---

35. www.bit.ly/33SVcTK, accessed 14th January, 2020.
36. www.bit.ly/3bvgadQ, accessed 14th January 2020.
37. www.bit.ly/2JrH2zo

about reading that Milton proposes which throws an especially bright spotlight on how reading is taught today:

> Next to make them expert in the usefullest points of Grammar, and withall to season them, and win them early to the love of vertue and true labour, ere any flattering seducement, or vain principle seise them wandering, some easie and delightful Book of Education would be read to them; whereof the Greeks have store, as Cebes, Plutarch, and other Socratic discourses ... But here the main skill and groundwork will be, to temper them such Lectures and Explanations upon every opportunity, as may lead and draw them in willing obedience, enflam'd with the study of Learning, and the admiration of Vertue; stirr'd up with high hopes of living to be brave men, and worthy Patriots, dear to God, and famous to all ages.[38]

Milton's project assumes educating boys (he has no time for girls of course) between the ages of 12 and 21 in 'a spatious house and ground about it fit for an Academy, and big enough to lodge a hundred and fifty persons, whereof twenty or thereabout may be attendants, all under the government of one',[39] so this vital, first 'easie and delightful Book of Education' is for those 12-year-olds. What's striking is that there is no list here. No need to steer a 12-year-old (boy or girl) through a lengthy catalogue of titles chosen because their authors specifically wrote to entertain the age group; no desire to match a list of books to their taste. Milton believes absolutely that the one great book is enough. There is no shortage, he says, after all, because in the end it is not the book which matters, but the teaching – 'the main skill and groundwork'. If you recall my description of how skilled English teachers conduct a lesson,[40] in which I talked about the *craft* of teaching and how adept English teachers are at provoking those they teach, you may start to see how Milton himself might have taught. The book is nothing without the teaching. It's just puritanical googling: information without knowledge.

---

38. John Milton, *Of Education*, www.bit.ly/2wEc2K1, accessed 15th January, 2020.
39. Ibid.
40. pp. 51-2.

Milton expects his teachers to enflame their pupils with 'the study of Learning' – to inspire them – and that happens through the interaction between them in the classroom. His teacher needs both the scholarship and the craft to deliver those 'Lectures and Explanations upon every opportunity'. It's a far cry from the kind of collaborative vision of teaching so common today, in which teachers work to create and share resources rather than to inspire or fuel a passion for learning in every child they teach. Milton's idea relies wholly on the ability of the child to sit with a book and engage their mind with that of the author.

A 2019 study for the Fordham Institute asked this pertinent question: 'Are the supplemental materials teachers download on popular websites high quality?'[41] The study concentrated on lesson plans and related materials for high school English language arts and includes this bleak statement: 'Sadly, the reviewers concluded that the majority of these materials are not worth using: more precisely, 64 percent of them should "not be used" or are "probably not worth using". On all three websites, a majority of materials were rated 0 or 1 on an overall 0–3 quality scale.'[42]

The study looked at over 300 of the most downloaded materials across three of the most popular websites which teachers use in the US: *Teachers Pay Teachers*, *ReadWriteThink* and *Share My Lesson*. There are, of course, similar popular sites in the UK. The study is unusually fair minded and the authors accept they cannot really know how the materials were used by teachers and appreciate teachers 'rarely use the materials as is'. I think this is equally true of textbooks and has been for many years. The value of textbooks themselves varies considerably according to the subject, but in my experience, it's unusual to find any skilled teacher who simply works through a textbook from cover to cover and thinks, 'job done'. Juxtaposing Milton's thoughts about reading with the Fordham Study's findings about using poorly designed lesson materials created by others exposes something significant about skilled, professional teaching.

If you break the whole business of lesson planning down to its basic components, most great lessons are built around an educational asset. In English, it's often textual, but it may be an image or even a physical object if the teacher believes it has the power to stimulate and interest the pupils.

41. Polikoff, Morgan with Jennifer Dean. (2019), *The Supplemental-Curriculum Bazaar: Is What's Online Any Good?* Washington, DC: Thomas B. Fordham Institute.

42. Ibid, p.5.

What matters is that the individual teacher chooses it because of where they are in the curriculum, with that particular class, and how effective they hope it will be in moving their learning forwards. I've delivered many hours of CPD to teachers, and a pointed instrument I'm fond of using is telling them, 'If kids walk out of the room not knowing more than when they walked in, you're not doing your job.' Frequently for English teachers, that asset is a specific book. The teacher selects a novel or poem, stage play or work of nonfiction because they know it and have faith in it. Only a foolish teacher, or a supply teacher being badly managed, tries to teach a text they don't know inside out themselves. But what I want to highlight is the distance between the modern practice of selecting a book and Milton's insistence that the choice is secondary to 'the main skill and groundwork' of exciting and engaging the pupils in learning. Think of how much time and effort goes into compiling age-appropriate reading lists in the hope children will work through them and learn something. Wouldn't teachers be better occupied expending energy in the classroom, in Milton's 'Lectures and Explanations upon every opportunity', the spoken English, the detailed vocabulary instruction and knowledge sharing that is both means and model for the pupils? A resource like Accelerated Reader looks at books as challenges to be worked through. It rewards children the more words and books they clock up, unsurprisingly reflecting the quantitative technology behind it.

I spent almost a decade in one school in which colleagues thought hard about choosing novels that would inspire and engage boys in those crucial first few years at secondary school. In all that time, I found only one book which I could almost guarantee would be well received. Knowing all I do now about real-world English, time spent reading and searching for that one book would have been far better utilised delivering the kind of intensely engaging lessons about any one of dozens of books that would have served the purpose just as Milton advocates, because the goal at that age is not to cover literary ground, but to create committed readers of books. Occasional or casual readers are never going to cover the literary ground anyway.

This is the pit into which young adult fiction falls. English teachers shouldn't confuse children reading for their own entertainment or pleasure with a professional need to inspire them as committed readers. For many teachers, choosing a class reader becomes difficult if the decoding ability of the class varies hugely. But this has to be balanced against the practical demand of teaching groups of children, not individuals. The job of teaching them to decode confidently is only a component part of the wider task of creating a classroom full of children who are able to sit alone somewhere, in silence, and focus their attention on the written thoughts of a writer they will almost certainly never meet, but whose ideas they must learn to engage with. Looked at in this way, that choice of text become less intimidating and important, once you embrace the idea of using it to do something much greater than merely ensuring it is read.

This suggests that one of the things English teachers can and should be doing is creating the ideal physical conditions for reading. That can apply both to books you read aloud to them and to books you expect them to read for themselves. Reading of both types is incompatible with noise or discomfort and there is plenty of scope for teachers to look at ways to ensure reading takes place regularly in ideal conditions. Do not fall for the multi-tasking myth. When technology businesses were busy belittling teachers as 'digital immigrants' while praising video-gaming teenagers as 'digital natives' (because it was a perfect opportunity to upsell entertainment products), I paid a visit to the Institute for the Future of the Mind at the University of Oxford to see how true this was and very quickly discovered that multi-tasking is a myth. If you're one of those undergraduates who sat up late reading about semiotics with your earphones on, trust me: it wasn't a good idea.

Putting all this together suggests that one of the most important decisions a teacher can make for this age group is choosing that conventional class reader. Not as you may think, because of a need to match the book to the children, but because it's absolutely central to your successfully creating those committed readers that you choose a book that inspires you to behave in the classroom in that model way Milton imagines. They need to experience a teacher whose knowledge, vocabulary and active mind is so visible, so effective at communicating ideas and provoking thought, that they are completely persuaded to become the committed readers we all know make successful school students. You need to embody for them the kind of knowledgeable, widely read, thoughtful, interesting adult that skilled reading nurtures.

None of this precludes teachers from talking about books and recommending books pupils might enjoy. What I'm suggesting pertains directly to that precious, limited time when they are all in front of you in lessons. Practically, how might this work in a real school? Once the English department has articulated its goals for reading clearly in its curriculum – so that every child knows why they are going to be given books to read; or asked to listen to teachers reading to them, or provided with silent, comfortable spaces to read in for extended periods – then each individual teacher needs to select that first 'easie and delightful Book of Education'. That's a big change for most, and discussing with colleagues what the choices might be would be wise, but it's crucial that the final choice remains the individual teacher's. Destroy that crucial link between a teacher and the assets they choose and you stifle their ability to teach well.

It's only fair that, having argued this case, I make a suggestion myself, and the one book I think I would choose that fits the bill and which I would be able to teach as effusively and expansively as I'm arguing for would be Bill Bryson's *Mother Tongue*. It sits well with work on linguistics and etymology happening simultaneously, and Bryson doesn't just share significant knowledge: he invites his reader to think for themselves about that knowledge. But the point of this exercise isn't to prescribe a single book to be taught; it's to define an educational goal to be achieved. Most skilled craftsmen own an elaborate and comprehensive toolset in which one chisel or hammer looks much like another to an outsider, but I'm willing to bet they reach for their favourites for excellent reasons.

I'm acutely aware that my reasoning about reading appears to marginalise the fiction or poetry that is, let's face it, currently the core of most English teaching in these early secondary school years. I stressed, when discussing writing, that real-world English teachers should not be in the business of teaching kids how to be poets or novelists. But reading fiction and poetry is not the same as trying to write it. Poems and novels are no different to the music or art other teachers introduce to children as aesthetically and culturally significant artefacts to be admired and enjoyed in their own right. Where I think we have gone seriously wrong is in regarding fiction or poetry, even drama, *primarily* as prompts to written work by pupils. That conventional lesson sequence that introduces pupils to a piece of fiction or poetry before asking them to use it as a model or to mimic it is, I think, wildly out of sync with today's world. I don't object at all to teaching children something about writing fiction, poetry or even drama, but it would be far better done outside of the formal English curriculum and within a creative framework that embraces art, music and theatre. Nonfiction writing has a far stronger claim on English lesson time in the real world.

Walk into any secondary English book cupboard and the proportion of fiction, poetry and drama to nonfiction will be around 10:1 – that is if you can find any nonfiction there at all that doesn't come pre-packaged inside a textbook. Everything I'm suggesting has major budgetary as well as curriculum and classroom implications. Where fiction is offered in the classroom, we need to be clear why and what we hope to achieve by putting it there. It isn't good enough to expect them to read a complete novel by H.G. Wells, Geraldine McCaughrean or Michael Morpurgo and then ask them, in effect, to try to copy some aspect of their professional prose. Why would they? There is nothing authentic about such a task. We need real clarity about where the value lies in reading novels at this age.

What we should be hoping to do is teach them how to lose themselves in a fictional world, to suspend their real lives for short periods of time and surrender their imagination to the gifts of a skilled storyteller. Some children entering secondary school might already be there, but most won't. They will need guidance and the right conditions to learn how to focus completely on the written prose in front of them so that they can enter the lives of the characters and the flow of the narrative, free from everyday childish concerns or anxieties.

Central to this job is being able to identify what barriers individuals face. For some, it will be all about decoding words and 'catching up' with the curriculum's expectations of them; for others it will be about the absence of prior knowledge that the novelist just assumed would be there. All need an explanation. We need to spell out to them why we have given them this book, why we want them to read it cover to cover and how that experience fits into their wider educational trajectory. Reading fiction successfully, surrendering yourself to someone else's thought through their prose, is the foundation stone on which all successful future reading is built. Children who never develop the habit may well succeed at school academically and even in employment, but their ability to assimilate knowledge, to consider new ideas and information from their reading, will always be limited by that inability to step out of the real world and into someone else's shoes. They may become hugely successful in life but they will never become successful scholars. For this reason, it's crucial that a breadth of reading is encouraged; but using up lesson time reading a wide range of texts, hoping breadth and variety alone will produce those committed readers you want to create, wastes time better spent on that primary goal in the more direct, classroom manner I've already described. Choose that one key book to deliver the primary goal, then recommend or use others to embed the habit.

Poetry reading, however, is a special case. When I wrote *The Point of Poetry*,[43] I stepped away from studies I'd previously written about poetry for students in order to focus on that army of adult metrophobes I'd met in the real world. People who passed their exams, went to university, held down well-paid, demanding jobs, who even spent some of their salary in Waterstones, but whose lifelong relationship with poetry was strictly Bad Samaritan: they pass it by on the other side of the road. In the end, I concluded that poetry actually had a central and hugely significant role to play in the English curriculum because, putting aside all questions of beauty or art, poetry is every languages' laboratory. It's where human beings test the boundaries of language to breaking point. It can't happen in prose. Studying poetry teaches you something unique. It teaches you what words can and cannot do. No one who studies it successfully succumbs unknowingly to the linguistic manipulation that successful advertising, marketing and (increasingly) the media and politics rely on. Poetry is the stockade every civilisation erects against barbarity. When are children ever taught that? Why do so many children leave school genuinely hating poetry? I'd argue that it's precisely because of the deeply entrenched creative imbalance, the post-'60s burden placed on poetry as personal therapy or activism, because too many teachers have fallen for the idea that it's part of the job to encourage children to express their passion, concern or anger. It really isn't. Not in the real world.

The English Association, founded in 1906 by scholars and English teachers to develop English studies in schools, publishes a magazine: *The Use of English*. One recent article in it is called, rather usefully for me, '"Real English" Versus "Exam English" – the Case for Authentic Experience of the Subject'.[44] From the title, I think it's reasonable to

---

43. Nutt, Joe. (2019) *The Point of Poetry*, Unbound.
44. www.bit.ly/2JsjYAJ, accessed 22nd January 2020.

expect a discussion connecting real-world English with what is taught in schools; but instead, what you find is an academically ring-fenced approach to the subject. English is treated in ivory-towered isolation from pupils' lived experience of it. The author even refers to the 'life cycle of English as a subject (from school to university to degree to PGCE and back into school)' before offering a description of what the entire English curriculum should be about 'at KS3, as well as at GCSE and A Level'. I've reproduced this description in full because it's so obviously relevant:

> Just as a mathematician (obviously) doesn't learn all the (infinite) answers to all the. [sic] (infinite) mathematical problems but ways of thinking about and solving them, and just as a geographer learns to think about space and locations in certain specific ways, so English teaches students to think 'as' critics. This may once have been, but is not [sic] longer, a sort of monolithic, fixed identity; it is no longer. Rather, it is a mobile, developing sense of a range of questions and ideas about the literary, widely defined, and [...] characterized by dissensus. Learning to 'think as a critic' is a process, which is why the second part of [*Doing English*] introduces long-standing debates and disagreements that have shaped the discipline and how it thinks: over value and the canon, understanding Shakespeare, authorial intention, figural language, narrative and creative writing.[45]

I have no quarrel with this as a definition of what it means to study English in higher education (apart from being, I think, justly unimpressed by the poor editing and literal nonsense it produces in an article about scholarly English). My chief concern is that this is seen as the purpose of studying English at school 'at KS3, as well as at GCSE and A Level'. When the author continues, the reason for this becomes clear. The same ideologically determined view of teaching as a profession I identified in chapter one is to blame. So 'When students of all ages learn about poetry, they should be engaging with the big and exciting ideas about

---

45. Ibid. (quoting Eaglestone, Robert., (2017) *Doing English: A Guide for Literature Students*, Fourth Edition (London: Routledge) p.18.)

what poetry is and what it can do' is closely followed by 'They should read widely, read diverse texts and – as the American educationalist Arthur N. Applebee has said so eloquently – understand much more about the canon by seeing it freshly, through the lens of other, diverse cultures and traditions.'[46] These are political objectives masquerading as educational ones. What could better illustrate the dramatic mismatch, described in chapter one, between the real world of English usage and how schools actually teach it?

Nonetheless, reading, listening to and teaching poetry does have a place at every stage of a secondary school pupil's education. It should occupy considerable lesson time in these first few years; but, most importantly, pupils also need to be taught why it matters. Alongside lessons aimed at nurturing their ability to listen to spoken English and detect the games poets play with sound – lessons that embed basic concepts like rhythm and rhyme – they need lessons that explain the part poetry plays in the development of their linguistic knowledge and experience. They need to know that studying it empowers them linguistically, that hearing, seeing, feeling and understanding what great poets do with words sharpens their own linguistic aptitude. They should be taught that the ability to 'appreciate' poetry – to identify, grasp and explain the artistry at work in it – has a profound impact on their own relationship with the English language. That poetry has a purpose greater than the sum of its words.

If you are going to do this well then considerable thought and care should go into selecting the poets and poems you teach because the risk of facing your pupils with hurdles that are too high is real. Poetry is difficult to write and difficult to study. As in every curriculum, sequencing matters. Far better to spend the first two years enjoying and fully understanding the mechanics of narrative verse by poets like Lewis Carroll or Edward Lear, for example, than forcing young teenagers into 'engaging with the big and exciting ideas' of contemporary poets. There is also an obvious connection to be made with the work on linguistics and etymology happening at the same time, so using verse examples from Old or Middle English where you can pick out macaronic techniques or teach them what alliteration is would be ideal. The curriculum should

---

46. Ibid.

be aiming to deliver texts that parallel linguistic work passing on knowledge about the history of English and its relationship with other languages. There's plenty of scope for conveying invaluable knowledge about religion, history and cultural attitudes in almost any Medieval verse, whether you choose something by the Gawain Poet or William Langland or introduce them to Chaucer. This is one of those rare occasions where the technology is a huge help because it isn't too difficult to find audio versions of older verse online. Few English teachers will be expert readers of Old or Middle English, but a word of warning from someone who has listened to a lot of online poetry performances. It's difficult to believe, but there is a surprisingly large cohort of poetry fans who themselves somehow bunked off all lessons about listening to poetry. An audio version online might look as though it comes from a perfectly credible source; but the second you start to listen, what you actually get is an unnatural, monotonous, portentous drawl, as though all computers come with a 'poetic voice' function that renders even the most mellifluous verse cacophonous. Even published poets aren't immune to this paradoxical malady.

How often do pupils studying A level literature find themselves encountering Chaucer for the very first time and having simultaneously to assimilate swathes of knowledge about the nature of the world he lived in because this is the first occasion they've heard his name? By the time pupils reach the final years of secondary school, their English curriculum should have provided them with a fundamental timeline they can confidently refer to. More often, they find themselves scrambling around to score contextual knowledge points because they don't own a clear, detailed enough picture of the period in which the text concerned was written. It has to be a warning that something's wrong when GCSE students studying *A Christmas Carol* have an image of Victorian London that includes cars and the internet. Similarly, they should know that the sound of English has changed dramatically over the centuries and not be overly concerned when faced with unfamiliar spellings or foreign words. Every English teacher will be familiar with another curious warning that the curriculum isn't what it should be. It's common for a child to be reading aloud perfectly fluently from a text, when the sudden appearance of a French or Spanish word hits them a smack in the face and they suddenly turn into

Stanley Unwin,[47] even though later the same day they'll be sitting in a French or Spanish class along the corridor.

Before I turn to GCSEs, let's revisit real-world English for a moment and acknowledge that not all educated adults possess similar reading skills. Someone who has spent several years steeped in sophisticated fiction or poetry reads in a markedly different way from someone whose undergraduate reading experience was restricted to scientific journals or theory, philosophy or social science. That should be the huge advantage every English teacher carries in their bloodstream. Working for a US client not long ago, I was on a video conference call with a team of colleagues putting together an outline for commercial bid. The team were using a slideshow as a template provided by the company to guide the process, but a few slides in the discussion faltered, then started to go round and round in circles. The warning signal for me was hearing specific phrases being repeatedly used, because people were clearly unsure of what they meant. Each slide had bullets with verbal prompts, and the notes underneath explained in greater detail what was to go into them. I read and reread one note in particular and after a few minutes intervened to check everyone's understanding of it. It wasn't especially clear prose, but it formed a clear instruction, and once I had run through it with everyone and reworded it, the flood gates opened and we had the job done shortly afterwards. I've no doubt it was the breadth of my literary reading experience and skill that allowed me to see what a team of highly educated young business colleagues could not.

I've devoted the first part of this chapter to what happens before pupils start studying for their GCSEs, the summative exams all 16-year-olds take in England. Currently, there is a lively and public dispute taking place between the schools inspectorate, Ofsted, and two of the largest multi-academy trusts in England who believe that Ofsted is punishing them for teaching GCSEs over three years instead of two. The trusts maintain that the high proportion of disadvantaged pupils in their schools requires them to do everything they can to maximise their exam success, because their pupils have nothing else to fall back on. They are disproportionately damaged by exam failure or poor performance.

---

47. For the unfamiliar, Unwin was a comedian with a unique gift for mangling the English language. 'Are you all sitty comftybold two-square on your botty? Then I'll begin' was his way of starting a story.

Increasing numbers of school leaders in such schools have even begun referring disparagingly to the kind of curriculum thinking Ofsted is encouraging as 'middle class' in an effort to counter the chief inspector's assertion that 'Grades are hollow if they don't reflect a proper education underneath.'[48] Yet Amanda Spielman, the chief inspector, gave even more power to her inspectors' elbows when she added: 'We should not incentivise apparent success without substance. This doesn't represent a good education for any child. And for those who aren't being read a different story every night, who aren't taken to the museum at the weekend, who don't get the chemistry set for Christmas, it is especially impoverished. These children need and deserve a proper, substantial, broad education for as long as schools have them.'[49]

GCSE English and English Literature

The trusts' strategy is curiously self-defeating: on the one hand, asking that everyone acknowledge the particular difficulties they face because of the disadvantaged communities from which they draw their pupils; while on the other, dismissing the educational goals they ruthlessly focus on (*because* they are the keys to success for their pupils) as inappropriately 'middle class'. It's the kind of impossible situation schools and teachers inevitably find themselves in when they fail to distinguish between educational and political goals. A healthier approach would be to reject entirely the fool's errand heaped on them by politicians to deliver social mobility, something schools can never achieve,[50] and focus their energy on what they *can* achieve: a high-quality schooling experience for all pupils, regardless of their social background. If they must stray into politics, then they should turn politicians' attention to the pre-school years on which so much of any school's success relies, regardless of class.

The curriculum I've been describing in the previous pages has consciously been for children in the first three years of secondary school. If there is one thing that repeatedly struck me when researching this book,

---

48. www.bit.ly/2WW1PDf, accessed 22nd January 2020.

49. Ibid.

50. Goldthorpe, John., Bukodi, Erzsébet., (2018) *Social Mobility and Education in Britain: Research, Politics and Policy,* CUP.

it's been just how extraordinarily imbalanced the teaching of English is for these children. An imbalance that GCSE entrenches for good. If you are an English teacher, and were asked to divide your school's pre-GCSE curriculum up into skills and knowledge, I wonder what the proportions would be? When children are asked to write, how often is their knowledge being tested compared to their creative writing skills? Skills they will never be required to demonstrate in adult life. When they are asked to read, how often is that reading specifically chosen in order to enhance their knowledge of the English language? Or is it just further literary reading? After three (or, in some cases, only two) years, this skills imbalance becomes irrecoverable; and if we put English literature to one side, studying English for most 16-year-olds in the UK is almost entirely a matter of skills.

Let's start with one of the most popular exam boards, AQA.[51] Pupils take two papers. The first is called 'Explorations in Creative Writing and Reading'. The board explicitly tells teachers, 'The aim of this paper is to engage students in a creative text and inspire them to write creatively themselves' before adding they must do this by demonstrating two things:

- 'in section A, reading a literature fiction text in order to consider how established writers use narrative and descriptive techniques to capture the interest of readers'
- 'in section B, writing their own creative text, inspired by the topic that they have responded to in section A to demonstrate their narrative and descriptive skills in response to a written prompt, scenario or visual image'

It couldn't be clearer. What teachers must do if they want their pupils to succeed is teach them to be creative writers. The only knowledge about English tested is their knowledge about 'narrative and descriptive techniques' used predominantly by creative writers.

The second paper is called 'Writers' Viewpoints and Perspectives', and the board tells teachers its aim is 'to develop students' insights into how writers have particular viewpoints and perspectives on issues or themes

---

51. www.bit.ly/3dNVHDh, access 23rd January 2020.

that are important to the way we think and live our lives'. As with paper one, it is primarily skills that are being assessed:

It will encourage students to demonstrate their skills by:

- in section A, reading two linked sources from different time periods and genres in order to consider how each presents a perspective or viewpoint to influence the reader
- in section B, producing a written text to a specified audience, purpose and form in which they give their own perspective on the theme that has been introduced to them in section A

Paper two has a nonfiction focus illustrated by this account of the kinds of texts pupils can expect to be required to answer questions on: 'Choice of genre will include high quality journalism, articles, reports, essays, travel writing, accounts, sketches, letters, diaries, autobiography and biographical passages or other appropriate non-fiction and literary non-fiction forms.' Which is admirably broad and, as they can be drawn from 'the 19th century, and either the 20th or 21st century', anyone would be forgiven for thinking that a pupil following this course could expect to experience an impressive range of reading material. If you bundle the phrase 'high quality journalism' in with the rest, there are ten different prose formats here. AQA's own examples of schemes of work are notably thin in this respect and under the 'Reading' column offer teachers no more advice than 'focus on prose fiction extracts or produce own set of linked literary non-fiction and non-fiction sources'.

In reality, when you look at schemes of work and resources teachers themselves design and share and the discussions teachers have amongst themselves, the focus is almost always on the skill and not the text. Teachers invest considerable time and energy in showing pupils how to answer the specific types of question, in teaching them the method, at the expense of the breadth of reading experience the exam specification implies. Scaffolding is everything; but as so many discussions between anxious teachers approaching the exam season indicate, what people keep finding is that it's all scaffolding and no building. The space where the child's writing needs to go remains empty because they haven't been taught to think for themselves. All the teaching effort has been directed at how to *write*, not how to *think*. The mechanics have replaced the engineers. I recently saw a resource in which one of these exam questions had been broken down into suggested topics for individual paragraphs, each one with a clear instruction written by the teacher onto a colour-coded printed sheet, so that all the pupil had to do was cross-reference their sheet with the specific passage they were being asked to write about and fill in the spaces.

This issue is exacerbated when you look at the way examiners think of nonfiction texts. Although each paper has a different title, there is essentially minimal difference in the way they treat the extracts they want pupils to write about. Newspaper or magazine articles are selected then queried in paper two, so that pupils can demonstrate not just a level of understanding, but knowledge about the mechanics of prose construction, in much the same way that creative extracts are chosen for paper one. To be deliberately reductive about it, 'Explorations in Creative Writing and Reading' deals with imaginative fiction, whereas 'Writers' Viewpoints and Perspectives' handles argument and opinion. Yet both ask pupils to show their level of understanding by identifying technique before demonstrating their own writing skills, chiefly by being invited not to write, but to mimic.

Go deeper into this and look at the specific written tasks pupils have to carry out from past papers, and the knowledge skills imbalance is striking. Here is a brief list of previous questions selected from AQA English papers one and two, sections A and B, that illustrates dramatically the narrowness of what is really being assessed.

- 'This text is from the middle of a short story. How has the writer structured the text to interest you as a reader?'
- 'A student said, "This part of the story, where the men encounter the Tyrannosaurus Rex, shows Eckels is right to panic. The Monster is terrifying!" To what extent do you agree?'
- 'Both sources describe the similar ways in which drivers behave. Use details from **both** sources to write a summary of what you understand about the similar behaviour of the drivers.'
- 'How does the writer use language to describe her first experiences of cycling?'
- 'Compare how the writers convey their similar perspectives on cycling in the city.'

- '"Cars are noisy, dirty, smelly and downright dangerous. They should be banned from all town and city centres, allowing people to walk and cycle in peace." Write a letter to the Minister for Transport arguing your point of view on this statement.'
- 'Write a story about a time when things turned out unexpectedly.'
- 'Your local newspaper is running a creative writing competition and the best entries will be published.'

Is this a world of English usage you recognise? The kind of person who writes letters to the Minister of Transport is probably on a police watch list. When was the last time you even saw a local newspaper that had genuine articles in it, never mind a creative writing competition? This analysis exposes how a critical summative exam comes to dominate children's experience of English as a subject in school. Teachers who are acutely aware that their own performance is being evaluated by the performance of the children they teach understandably trim away anything they judge will detract from what the pupil needs to be able to do in the exam room. They are completely conscious that those they teach will be assessed overwhelmingly on the skills they have and not the knowledge they pass onto them. This is precisely how GCSE tyrannises the wider, richer curriculum all good schools aim to deliver.

If we look at another popular exam board, OCR, we see a similar picture. The specification for OCR's latest English Language GCSE[52] tells teachers that studying it will encourage pupils to:

- 'Develop independent and critical thinking.'
- 'Engage with the richness of our language and literary heritage.'
- 'Experiment in writing across a range of contexts and styles.'

In a section usefully called 'What are the key features of this specification?', OCR provide more detail than AQA but essentially the same skills are being tested. One paper (01) is called 'Communicating information and ideas', while the second (02) is 'Exploring effects and impact'. Their list of likely set texts is shorter and includes only 'prose fiction, journalism, travel writing and biographical writing'; but when you look at what the written

---

52. www.bit.ly/2wGVyAQ, accessed 23rd January 2020.

tasks are, they are very familiar. Pupils are expected to develop 'creative and imaginative writing skills and the ability to write accurately for a range of purposes and audiences, using their understanding of linguistic and literary methods'. There are similar questions to assess pupils' understanding of specific passages that focus on structure, inference, vocabulary and effects, but the difference between the two extended written tasks is more clear cut than AQA. The (01) paper stipulates that, 'The writing tasks will have a clear audience and purpose and be written in a non-fiction form'; while (02) is even more unequivocal, stating simply, 'The focus is on creative writing.'

At the risk of putting the drumstick right through the skin of the drum, why do we ask children to do this when only a handful of them will ever need to, yet tens of thousands will spend many hours in employment having to write articulately, accurately, fluently and often at length?

Both boards are to a large degree constrained by Ofqual's assessment objectives, which are mandatory, so it's only fair that we spend some time looking thoughtfully at them. They will be familiar to English teachers but here they are (excluding the three relating to spoken English, which I will deal with later):

- AO1:
  - Identify and interpret explicit and implicit information and ideas.
  - Select and synthesise evidence from different texts.
- AO2: Explain, comment on and analyse how writers use language and structure to achieve effects and influence readers, using relevant subject terminology to support their views.
- AO3: Compare writers' ideas and perspectives, as well as how these are conveyed, across two or more texts.
- AO4: Evaluate texts critically and support this with appropriate textual references.
- AO5: Communicate clearly, effectively and imaginatively, selecting and adapting tone, style and register for different forms, purposes and audiences. Organise information and ideas, using structural and grammatical features to support coherence and cohesion of texts.
- AO6: Candidates must use a range of vocabulary and sentence structures for clarity, purpose and effect, with accurate spelling and punctuation. (This requirement must constitute 20% of the marks for each specification as a whole.)

With the exception of the spoken word skills that are non-examined, these six statements capture the entirety of the English knowledge and skills we expect 16-year-olds to master. (Teachers will also know that the assessment weighting favours AO5 and AO6.) They are in themselves admirably succinct definitions of things we want children to be able to do; apart from the implication in AO2 that pupils must possess knowledge in the shape of 'subject terminology', all the emphasis is on the skills they can demonstrate. What's missing is a shared and clear understanding of the knowledge they need to develop those skills. That's what you would expect a well-designed key stage 3 English curriculum to contain, but how often is that the case? It's far more likely that, as in the case argued by the two multi-academy trusts I referred to earlier, the GCSE tail is wagging the key stage 3 dog. More pertinently, neither has much to do with the real world.

Imagine instead that during key stage 3, besides having the foundational knowledge about linguistics, orthography and etymology I discussed earlier in this section, pupils were regularly shown videos of meetings or conversations and asked to record what is being said. Imagine they were given lots of examples of colloquial English, in video or audio form as well as written, and asked to render them in formal English. Imagine if they were shown examples of people communicating badly, of good and poor debates, or were taught how to describe a step-by-step process or prioritise information according to changing criteria. These are just a few of the kinds of activities which would better reflect what they would be doing with the English language when they leave school. Schools don't have to submit to the tyranny of GCSE.

There's one part of GCSE English that I've deliberately left until this point because it's the one most closely connected to the real world. All GCSE English specifications now include spoken English. AQA describe it like this:

> The aim of the assessment is to allow students to demonstrate their speaking and listening skills by:
>
> - giving a presentation in a formal context
> - responding appropriately to questions and to feedback, asking questions themselves to elicit clarification
> - using spoken Standard English.

In section one, I discussed how important presentations were in the real world. No one should underestimate how much this matters because for every pupil who ends up publishing a short story, poem or writing a novel, there will be those same tens of thousands who have to stand up in front of an audience and present their own or their employer's ideas, week after week. Although mandatory, and all the GCSE awarding bodies have essentially the same requirements, this aspect of studying GCSE is non-examined and most pupils are assessed internally by their teachers using criteria that focus on intelligibility and formal language use. From everything I've argued up to this point, you might expect me to be clamouring for spoken English to be examined, for it to play a much larger part in the awarding of a GCSE in English, but I was still teaching the last time oral English was examined at GCSE.

In conventional schools, where English teaching is timetabled and children are taught in large groups in dedicated lessons, it's extremely difficult to examine this kind of work for the simple reason that, like playing a musical instrument, it's hugely time consuming. Children working their way through grades 1–8 in the UK's music examination system not only have frequent, dedicated, one-to-one tuition by an instrumentalist, they take their exams in front of external examiners, often having to travel and miss part of their routine timetable to do so. None of that infrastructure is available to English teachers trying to teach a class of 30 individuals how to deliver an effective presentation to an audience. All kinds of shortcuts were inevitable, and when I did this kind of work, it wasn't unusual for an oral assessment to consist of a series of group discussions, happening simultaneously in the same room and lesson, while the teacher moved from one group to another and tried to listen in 'live' to carry out the assessment. The opportunity cost of organising 30 unique presentations during timetabled English lessons is simply prohibitive. Years of doing that kind of work also taught me that no matter how detailed the criteria or how meticulously you try to follow them, when dealing with teenagers, what you really ended up assessing was not spoken English, but their natural confidence. Whatever type of formal assessment I designed and ran, they were entirely superficial exercises and were inevitably influenced by everything else I knew about an individual pupil from my general teaching of them.

None of that undermines the necessity of teaching pupils how to deliver an effective presentation. Even if at times you know all you are doing is addressing varying degrees of confidence. In fact, that teenage reality reinforces the argument that it should feature as an important part of the curriculum well *before* 16-year-olds find themselves rushing through a hastily put together recording session predominantly for the benefit of an external examiner. It requires English departments to think carefully through what knowledge pupils need, how to teach it, and how to ensure everything necessary is covered. It's not simply a matter of teaching them how to use PowerPoint. It's a much more sophisticated challenge. More significantly, whatever techno zealots say or however colourful and tempting the animation software, it's a linguistic challenge. Here are the three missing assessment objectives for spoken English:

- AO7: Demonstrate presentation skills in a formal setting.
- AO8: Listen and respond appropriately to spoken language, including to questions and feedback on presentations.
- AO9: Use spoken Standard English effectively in speeches and presentations.

Oddly enough, the word that carries the greatest challenge there is 'Listen'. In chapter one, I pointed out that the rise of social media meant teaching children how to listen had become 'a contemporary imperative'. Recent political events – certainly in the UK, where the Brexit vote, the antagonistic reaction it provoked and the fiercely fought general election it eventually resulted in galvanised an entire electorate – demonstrate how important information is to a healthy democracy. The entire 'fake news' phenomenon, designed to censor, intimidate and prohibit, is itself ironically indicative of healthy democratic discourse because it unintentionally placed a premium on listening. Information is valueless until someone listens.

It's too little and too late to think you can cover this vital aspect of modern English usage by adding it to a summative exam while surrounding it with messages that tell teachers and pupils it's so unimportant that it's not even examined. Spoken English should be woven throughout the entire secondary school curriculum, embracing everything from the most practical – teaching children how to deliver an effective presentation – to the most aesthetic – teaching them how to listen to, read and enjoy great poetry. Teachers should also be entirely clear what it is they are teaching pupils to do when delivering on that dangerously vague Ofqual AO8 instruction, 'respond appropriately'. 'Appropriate', like 'phobia' and 'offensive', is a regular ingredient of contemporary word salad. These are words that signal evasiveness or censorship in contemporary debate far more often than a willingness to listen. For many people, they are the verbal equivalent of sticking your fingers in your ears while drowning out someone else's voice with a stream of gibberish.

All a teacher should be looking for from a child who is responding 'appropriately' is clear evidence not only that they heard what was said accurately but also that their response either enhances or refutes what was said to them. What it certainly does not mean is that the listener responds merely by issuing or repeating a predetermined statement, probably the most common strategy used by politicians, pundits and others regularly making an appearance in our media.

The more you look at GCSE English, the more you find yourself asking what valuable educational purpose it now serves. Is it really that twin educational pillar (along with maths) that it's sold to parents, the general public and employers as? For many teachers, not just English teachers, teaching exam technique is a sensible and important part of the job. They think about it carefully and discuss it with colleagues; most will have favourite tips and ideas of their own they have faith in. When I was still teaching, I remember being impressed by some research I read on the psychology of exams that argued that, in essence, students who were the most successful at taking exams shared one distinctive characteristic. They approached the event as what the researchers called a 'cumulative' experience. That is, instead of walking into the school's dining room clutching a pen, a calculator and a cuddly toy with some vague aspiration in their head of passing or even of achieving a specific grade, what they did was calmly sit down and approach the whole experience as one in which the object of the game was to accumulate marks. They looked at the first question and if it said '5 marks', they consciously reframed the question in their head as, 'What do I need to do to gain 5 marks?' If it said '20 marks', their thought process would be, 'What do I need to do to gain 20 marks?' As they proceeded through the exam, they built up a sense of what they had accomplished one question at a time. The research seemed, to me at the time, entirely credible, and I would add this was more than 20 years before I'd ever heard of the researchED movement or found myself regularly speaking at their conferences. More mundanely, like many other teachers I'm sure, I told those I taught that the best thing they could take into any examination room, besides a well-prepared mind, was a highlighter pen.

Looking at the advice and strategies English teachers offer pupils today, what strikes me most of all is how dramatically farther down the exam technique route schools have travelled. When I first started working in business, I had to assimilate an entirely new vocabulary, and one of the terms I kept hearing, which as a teacher I was completely unfamiliar with, was 'risk'. It's an extremely useful concept in business and one which has all kinds of relevant applications. Today, when I look at the way English teachers invest considerable time and energy searching for and creating resources, what I see is them trying to remove as much risk as possible for their pupils in the exam room. This has become such a dominant strategy that exam technique has become exam rehearsal. As is so often the case, what is only sensible and prudent in a business context has some profoundly damaging side effects in education.

Instead of pupils being taught a carefully thought-through sequence of significant cultural knowledge about the English language, and skills in parallel – which together prepare them for a summative exam – what we have is a situation where knowledge is taught only if it can be seen to support the specific, narrow set of skills examined. Hence the emphasis placed on identifying technique and structure, as well as mimicking them. This is *training* pupils in English, not teaching them. If they sit down in a GCSE exam room and replicate a series of steps and activities they have been taught, irrespective of the content in the questions they are asked, have they really been taught about the English language or have they merely been taught one way to take a test? This is precisely why so many pupils perform well in those English literature exams when they haven't even read the set texts. They've been trained to.

This urge to scaffold every imaginable task is equally treating a symptom, not offering a cure. Every pupil sitting in an English examination room faced with a written task is being asked to think for themselves. The prose they write can only ever be a more or less accurate reproduction of the thinking they've done, even when that only involves them remembering what they've been told to reproduce. Because however much they might like to, teachers can't take the exam for their students. That's called cheating. If teaching in the years preceding summative testing focused on strategies to enable and develop their capacity and ability for thought – to make it a natural, even an enjoyable response they anticipate with pleasure, not fear or anxiety – it's not difficult to imagine the likely difference in their final exam performance.

The forgotten third

Which brings me onto one of the most irritably resistant issues about teaching English for the real world. In any norm-referenced exam, such as GCSE English, what many current campaigners like to call 'the forgotten third' will be condemned to failure every year. If the bell curve tolls for anyone, it tolls for them. No matter how skilful the teaching, or brilliant the curriculum, a substantial number of 16-year-olds will always fall at the final hurdle and feel the marks on their shins for years to come. In 2019, the GCSE pass rate in English dropped below a third to 31.9%, with over 290,000 16-year-olds failing to achieve a grade 4. Current school improvement policy in the UK appears to imagine the bell curve slowly shuffling to the right and taking people along with it, in the hope that they are in reality somehow more skilled in English than earlier cohorts of children; but both human nature and experience suggest otherwise. Since 2016, it's also been mandatory for pupils who fail GCSE English in England to retake the exam, and consequently, for many, that just adds to the scar tissue on their shins. Those who achieve only the lowest grades (1 or 2) are now offered a functional skills qualification which, at the top level 2, is comparable to the GCSE pass level. The sensible and commendable idea is to ensure every child attains a personally valuable level of reading, writing and speaking in English, which the Department for Education spells out usefully for the purposes of this book as: 'Achievement of the qualification demonstrates the ability at an appropriate level to read, write, speak, listen and communicate in English, and to apply these skills effectively to a range of purposes in the workplace and in other real life situations.'[53]

There it is again: that real-world expectation, this time seasoned with that word salad regular, 'appropriate'. When you look at what pupils are

---

53. Department for Education, (2018) *Subject Content. Functional Skills, English*, p. 4.

tested on, the first and possibly unkind impression you're likely to get is that this is just a dumbed-down GCSE exam. The basic structure is the same, with half the paper containing questions about the workings of a prose extract to demonstrate candidates' reading ability, followed by questions designed to get them to write fluently and accurately themselves. When you look at the assessment criteria, words like 'varied', 'relevant' and 'occasionally' are used to distinguish the lowest levels from the 'complex', 'cogent', 'clearly' and 'persuasively' descriptors of a higher, level 2 performance, equivalent to a GCSE grade 4. From a real-world perspective, when I rooted around some past papers, I noted one question which asked pupils to read text from a web page, which at first sounds eminently real-world, until you consider those PISA figures I referred to earlier about teenagers and screen time, meaning such an unnatural activity would strike any teenager as decidedly odd. If it's a web page, it should work like a web page. Cutting and pasting the text just illustrates how far we have to go before examiners grasp how profoundly technology affects how language is used. Another question asking candidates to write an email displayed the same weakness because it asked them to reply, not to accept an offer of an interview for a job, but to apologise for not turning up to an interview. I defy anyone not to find that funny. What possible purpose such an email serves, I'll leave you to decide. Meanwhile, in the real world, entire books have been written on the arcane art of crafting emails to literary agents and publishers so that they might actually bother to reply.

However, that's an unfair overall judgement because other aspects of the functional skills course, notably reading and spelling, work hard to identify specific words and linguistic difficulties, like commonly con-fused homonyms, that would undoubtedly hinder any pupil's functioning in the real world. Clearly a lot of thought and effort has gone into identify-ing some of the most intransigent literacy problems 'the forgotten third' face. The question finally has to be: would the kind of real-world English curriculum focus and teaching I'm advocating reduce that worryingly persistent fraction even further? I've no doubt whatsoever that it would.

CHAPTER THREE
ENGLISH LITERATURE

The argument for teaching literature

In the preceding chapters, I offered only a few thoughts on teaching English literature in the first years at secondary school. In this third chapter, I'm going to focus entirely on English literature because at a time when politicians are all too eager to encourage more children, especially girls, to study STEM[54] subjects at school and into higher education (for entirely political but undoubtedly real-world reasons), it's vital to make the educational argument for the teaching of English literature.

The UK has a National STEM Learning Centre based at the University of York.[55] Besides two grants of over £3 million from the Department for Education and the Wellcome Trust in 2018, the organisation was granted £68 million by the Department for Education to establish a National Centre for Computing Education. It's the second national-level CPD project I have myself had a professional role in. It's a key part of the UK government's response to a widely reported skills shortage in STEM subjects highlighted by employers and universities. STEM Learning conducted research themselves in 2018[56] which identified a current shortfall of 173,000 skilled workers, and which found 89% of STEM businesses were struggling to recruit. STEM Learning replaced a previous quango, Becta, set up in 1998 to promote the effective use of

---

54. Science, Technology, Engineering and Mathematics.

55. STEM Learning is a joint initiative funded by the Department for Education, the Department for Business, Energy and Industrial Strategy, the Wellcome Trust and the Gatsby Charitable Foundation.

56. www.bit.ly/2WVwReB, accessed 28th January 2020. The research covered 400 HR Directors and business decision makers.

ICT in education. In 2010, it had an annual budget of £112.5 million and between 2002 and 2010 oversaw the spending of £1.5 billion on technology in schools. No other subjects studied in UK schools are given such generous support from central government. This level of subject-specific investment is merely the sharp end of that far wider technology pressure all schools and teachers have been placed under by the rapid expansion of the internet and other new technologies in the last two decades, most recently marketed by technology businesses and their heralds as 'the fourth industrial revolution'.

While investment has been made in STEM subject teaching, English teaching organisations have noted a distinct drop in the numbers of candidates studying English literature at A level and on into university. Some have joined the dots and claimed the drop is a direct result of the increasing numbers pupils, especially girls, choosing to study STEM subjects in order to secure a university place. JCQ, the Joint Council for Qualifications, reported a 31% drop in A level entries in English Language, English Literature, and the combined English Language and Literature exam between 2012 and 2019. EMC, the English and Media Centre, published the results of a survey[57] carried out in 200 schools that painted the same, disappointing picture. Their director, Andrew McCullum, was reported in *Tes* as saying, 'Policymakers need to wake up to the damage being done to our national subject. If they let the situation continue like this, then soon we will have a real crisis in recruitment to English teaching.'[58] The EMC have no hesitation in blaming Michael Gove's GCSE reforms for this apparent trend. One of their consultants, Barbara Bleiman, spelt this dissatisfaction out in the same *Tes* article: 'Historically, students have always loved English – it was often their favourite subject. Now they are turning away from it. Teachers say it is the "dry", "dull", "narrow" GCSEs, particularly English language, that are switching them off in droves.'[59]

Around a decade ago, I was commissioned by my employer to carry out a review of the research on 'excellent' secondary school teaching. The

57. www.bit.ly/2Uzrgco, accessed 28th January 2020.
58. www.bit.ly/2xEKDaK, accessed 28th January 2020.
59. Ibid.

choice of adjective is very important. It's not an over-researched field,[60] but after carrying out the work, I discovered there were really only two things people appeared to agree on that distinguished excellent teaching in the secondary school. The first was the depth of the teacher's subject knowledge, and the second was the 'passion' they exhibited for it. The same word, 'passion', made a notable appearance in different research. Shortly after writing up my research, I moved on from that employment and a few years later, after my ex-employer had also changed their CEO, was intrigued to see them publish research into 'effective' secondary school teaching, written by one of the external academics they regularly farmed research out to. A reminder, if one were needed, that sometimes, even single words carry substantial burdens. No subject is 'dry', 'dull' or 'narrow' unless a teacher makes it so. The EMC's complaints merely reflect their view of what the goal of teaching English should be.

One of the most dispiriting aspects of the contemporary educational world is the insistence by some teachers, teacher educators and even researchers that teaching children to read through synthetic phonics is, in some mysterious way, deeply detrimental. I'm not about to enter that debate here because it's akin to the attitude a minority of parents have displayed in recent years to vaccination programmes, the only real difference being that instead of kids dying, they just never learn to read. There is at least consensus about the need for children to learn to read if they are to succeed at school. Budgets, teacher time and considerable additional resources in secondary schools are invested in trying to bring that substantial number of pupils who still struggle to read to a point where they can participate in lessons. It's embarrassing to have to spell this out, but the attitude of some schools and teachers necessitates it. Secondary schools are highly conventional institutions. They can only function under three specific conditions. They need skilled, knowledgeable teachers, supportive parents and co-operative children. Where any one of these is missing or weak, a school is going to struggle. If the last one isn't there, you can have the most attractive, cleverly designed new building crammed with the latest technology costing millions, but no one should kid themselves that it's a school. I've visited a few that fall into this

60. One of the best pieces of research is Hattie, J.A.C. (2003, October). *Teachers make a difference: What is the research evidence?* Paper presented at the Building Teacher Quality: What does the research tell us ACER Research Conference, Melbourne, Australia.

unfortunate category. Children struggling to read in a secondary school are constantly faced, lesson after lesson, with an impossible hurdle. Poor behaviour in schools has, of course, a myriad of causes, many deeply personal and rooted in individual or group relationships because, as noted earlier, for children, schools are all about friendships. However, if you wanted to engineer into a school a means to provoke poor classroom behaviour, what better way to do it than to present a number of children in every lesson and every classroom with tasks they simply cannot do?

In the previous chapter, I wrote at length about reading and how schools and teachers should think about it, discuss it and nurture it in those first few important years of secondary education. I'll repeat why it's imperative this happens:

> Reading fiction successfully, surrendering yourself to someone else's thought through their prose, is the foundation stone on which all successful future reading is built. Children who never develop the habit may well succeed at school academically and even in employment, but their ability to assimilate knowledge, to consider new ideas and information from their reading, will always be limited by that inability to step out of the real world and into someone else's shoes. They may become hugely successful in life but they will never become successful scholars.[61]

Teaching literature is therefore inseparable from teaching English. Introducing children to the novel is a cornerstone of all English teaching, so it follows that teachers need to have some clear ideas about which novels and when. This is a thorny issue for children aged between about 11 and 14 because even though they may be skilled decoders of prose, they may not possess the self-discipline, breadth of vocabulary, cultural knowledge or imaginative capacity a specific novel requires. It's also far from straightforward to choose suitable novels for children at this age precisely because they are children and most canonical novels are written by adults for adults. There is, of course, a rich vein of children's fiction to mine; but the moment any teacher starts digging, they are faced with genre, and genre can so easily undo that prime aim of teaching a

---

61. See above, pp. 78–79

whole class of children how to lose themselves in an imaginative work of fiction. It's inevitable that whereas one child in a group might relish the magical world of C.S. Lewis or Ursula K. Le Guin, another will loathe it. While one may instantly respond to H.G. Wells's promise of time travel or interplanetary war, another may find it baffling. This is a perfectly reasonable argument for encouraging breadth of reading experience, but I think teachers might reduce the risk and prepare the ground better if they were far more explicit about the aim. Just as in the real world, the accompanying messages matter. English departments need to articulate for themselves why they are asking pupils to undertake the task of reading a complete novel before explaining those expectations to the children equally clearly. You might wish the entire work to be read in silence and independently. At the other end of the scale, you may even decide that reading the entire work aloud to them as a group will further your goal. Whatever the strategy, they need to know the goal. There's no reason that different classes in the same year group must read the same text. It's vital to maintain that relationship between the teacher and the educational asset they select, so different teachers may describe precisely the same goal while using different novels. Time spent defining and agreeing those goals, even the precise wording to be used, will be time well spent.

One of the main features of recent attempts at educational reform has been the way people have tried to transfer business practice into schools. It's been visible internationally in accountability initiatives and most obviously, in England at least, in the academisation programme where a few large academy chains have been led by individuals with considerable commercial experience. Not long after the £28 million National College of School Leadership (which someone who clearly had no military experience whatsoever dubbed 'Sandhurst for teachers') was established at the University of Nottingham in 2002, if you had visited their professional development website you would have found the 'most read' resource on there for trainee headteachers was advice cut and pasted directly from the *Harvard Business Review*. Whoever had done the pasting had not even bothered to delete the word 'profit'. This kind of naive transference didn't help anyone, but one thing successful businesses are extremely good at – and which is not at all difficult for English departments to mimic – is communications. Good businesses worry about the precise messages they wish to convey. They make sure that someone skilful crafts them and that employees use them. It really is worth the effort not just to agree your departmental goals, but to draft the precise wording to be used to convey them to others – most significantly, pupils – and insist that this is used and repeated.

You cannot force any child to immerse themselves in fiction by walking them through a long list of novels you chose for them in an attempt to cover the ground between Edith Nesbit and Malorie Blackman. You stand a far better chance if you tell them exactly what it is you want them to be able to do, and then provide the conditions for them to do it. It only takes one book to open the door to years of conversations about what to read next and why – the kind of discussion that paves the way for them to become discerning readers for life.

In terms of English literature, what also needs to happen quickly in secondary school is that alongside starting the development of the linguistic and historical timeline I described in chapter two, you need to begin teaching a parallel, literary timeline. This should start with the origins of drama, history and democracy in the classical world and cover early English and Medieval verse, Shakespeare and the Elizabethan theatre, Milton, the Restoration and Johnson's dictionary, the 18th century, Romantic poetry, the Victorian period and finally the 20th century. It's important to be realistic about the aims here, and not feel discouraged by the implied scale. What you want them to develop in the run up to GCSE is nothing more demanding than a clear sense of how the English language has itself changed over time, alongside selected great works of literature that exemplify that change. The concept of a dictionary – and key historical examples from John of Garland through Dr Johnson to the modern *OED* – needs to be introduced. They should know some of the key writers by name, have a clear sense of where they sit in relationship to one another historically, and ideally have been introduced to key texts from each period so that they have something more to refer to than a list of authors. Such a timeline should be as visible and common in English classrooms as the periodic table is in science.

To illustrate what this might mean, imagine a 16-year-old who has successfully assimilated such a timeline. Imagine showing them an extract from Sir Thomas Malory's *Le Morte Darthur,* anything from Shakespeare, something by Pope or Fielding, a slice of Keats, a few paragraphs from Hardy or George Eliot. Is it really too much to expect that they would be able to put them accurately in chronological order? This is significant knowledge they need to progress academically but also to be democratically free to think and choose for themselves, not least what subjects they might wish to continue to study in school and at university. They should learn to see literature as the beating heart of democratic thought. Woven into the literary timeline, there needs to be a key thread which traces freedom of expression and the crucial role specific authors and works have played in its shifting history. I'm not going to prescribe rigidly what that part of the curriculum should cover, not least because there is so much to choose from; but as an indication of the kinds of links that need to be drawn, here are some suggestions:

- The classical world of Socrates, his trial and execution
- Roman poets and censorship, perhaps through Ovid and his exile by Augustus
- The rise of printing and the Catholic Church's concern to restrict publication throughout the 16th century through the use of the *Index Librorum Prohibitorum*
- European governments' use of licensing laws to control what was published
- Elizabethan theatre, Shakespeare and the Master of the Revels
- The Star Chamber's role in limiting printing to the universities and the City of London
- Cromwellian censoriousness and Milton's great defence of free speech, *Areopagitica*
- The appearance of magazines like *Tatler* and *The Spectator* in the early18th century
- The impact of Darwin and evolution on Victorian morality
- The *Lady Chatterley* trial in 1928
- The fatwa issued against the novelist Salman Rushdie because of *The Satanic Verses*

One of the major risks of iconoclastic English teaching that emphasises pupils' creative writing is, ironically, that it leads to an erosion of freedom of expression. If you are repeatedly told that you and your words, no matter how shallow their conceptual foundations or ill-disciplined their shape, are all that matters, then we shouldn't be surprised when adults start redefining single words, even ones as biologically and culturally determined as 'woman', to suit their personal or political agenda. Forget what a lexicographer has to say; I say it means *this*. That's what really lies at the heart of our current cultural maelstrom. It falls to English teachers to redress this balance and restore some stability to language, otherwise we face a future reality as linguistically amorphous as anything written by Samuel Beckett or Harold Pinter.

This means that over those first three years at secondary school, pupils must be introduced to a series of famous writers and their work. Getting bogged down as a department in deciding who and what to study will be a distraction because what really matters is that the sequence is correct and that each individual teacher makes that crucial choice of the educational asset they want to teach around. NFER, the National Foundation for Educational Research, an organisation that has a declared interest in teacher welfare and success, has just published research which argues, 'Teachers' perceived autonomy over what they do in their jobs and how they do it is strongly associated with greater job satisfaction and intention to stay in the profession.'[62] Another good reason, were one needed, to insist on individual teachers choosing the novels, plays and poetry they teach.

In part, what I'm suggesting is a radical rethink about the literature teacher's relationship with their class. Excellent secondary teachers have both depth of knowledge and passion, and it's these two things pupils need their teachers to deliver. I've written extensively as a columnist about how schools and teachers have become the favourite playthings of politicians, celebrities and lobbyists. Anyone with a virtue to signal or a social conscience to parade regards schools as easy pickings. This anti-educational trend is so normalised, a colleague who works as an educational technology adviser for the World Bank told me a few years ago that he had grown weary of being approached by Silicon Valley millionaires in their twenties or thirties eager to spend some of their excess cash on improving education through technology, because it was happening so regularly. He is also a skilled and knowledgeable researcher so he always politely advised them to spend their money elsewhere. The organisation Parents and Teachers for Excellence started recorded news stories about such initiatives in 2018, and then again in 2019. It looks very much as

---

62. www.bit.ly/2xJwfOk, accessed 29th January, 2020.

though, overwhelmed by the flood, they abandoned the list in July 2019 when it stood at 114 different items.[63] Besides obvious popular choices like reducing knife crime and climate change, my personal favourites include a judge from TV's *Great British Bake Off* telling schools it's their responsibility to teach children all about food to counter the obesity crisis and the National Education Union calling for schools to teach children about breast ironing. It really is *Looking-Glass* time when the largest teacher union thinks its job is to prevent teachers from doing theirs.

Your passion for literature and the depth of your knowledge are, after all, things entirely within your control. Breast ironing and climate change aren't. Instead of feeling impelled to scaffold and support every step of a child's journey to a brief spell in a GCSE literature examination room, you should position yourself from the moment they enter the school not as their crutch, but as a model scholar. This doesn't necessitate a wholesale abandonment of tools and resources you have faith in. That positive relationship between the teacher and the asset is the kernel around which all curriculums are delivered. This is why using scripted lessons is training and not teaching. Unless the script leaves the key decision about material assets to the individual teacher, it will be someone else's lesson you are trying to teach. It does mean rethinking the levels of responsibility and initiative you should expect from pupils and what you can do to nurture scholarly practice in them.

This raises the key question of what constitutes subject knowledge in literary studies. Knowledge about any subject embraces more than the accumulated wisdom of generations of previous students and teachers. It begins with recognising, in conjunction with others, what it is you are studying. The focus in literature, since it became a distinct field of study in the Enlightenment, is on written work that through the passage of time, sometimes remarkably quickly, has achieved some degree of status through its artistic merit. It covers all forms of fiction, poetry and anything written for production in a theatre. In this sense, a libretto is literature, it's just not commonly studied as such. Subject knowledge doesn't stop there. To be a student of literature, you also need to learn *how* to study it, and this involves owning a toolset which, like all toolsets, has some ubiquitous, frequently employed things like textual analysis and a

---

63. www.bit.ly/3bO49R7, accessed 30th January 2020.

subject-specific vocabulary, together with new and as-yet-undiscovered tools because there is nothing carved in stone about any subject which has the pursuit of knowledge as its goal. Equipping those you teach with the most extensive, high-quality toolset you can is really the aim of anyone teaching literature in a secondary school setting. It is for scholars in universities to design the new tools.

I would advise any English department setting out to design a literature curriculum to do two key things. The first is to ignore the needs of the schools inspectorate. Under the new leadership of Amanda Spielman, Ofsted could not have spelled things out more clearly that it does not want its processes to generate work in schools that distracts teachers from their job teaching children. School leaders obviously play a part in this, but sitting down to draft and compile a complex document – the only purpose of which is to demonstrate to an inspector, who spends a few hours at most in your school, that you are following a specific curriculum – is an opportunity cost those you teach can't afford. The second thing is to think in terms of that high-quality toolset. What is it precisely you want them to own so that they can function as students of literature? A helpful simplification of that question might be: what is it that you know how to do and which you want them to know how to do too? I'll pick up that key question after dwelling a little on the role of the school library. In the real world, public libraries have suffered something of an identity crisis. Hit by funding challenges and attacked as redundant by techno-zealots who continue to peddle the lie that information equals knowledge, or that we all carry a library around on our phones, many libraries have responded by cutting services, or trying to reinvent themselves as internet cafes with books. The 'Famous Author Defends Libraries' news story has become a cliché and, like all clichés, is consequently impotent. It's a tragedy that these hugely important educational resources have become a victim of inept politics. Championed by the liberal left far more for their potential to characterise their political opponents as uncaring barbarians than because they themselves truly appreciate them as educational resources of huge value, libraries are in turn starved of investment or thoughtlessly automated, depending on whose grasping fingers are on the purse strings.

Meanwhile, in the real world, climate change has added considerable weight to a ubiquitous political and media message which sees the future as an extraordinarily complex problem to be magically solved by educated men and women without the aid of books. There is a whole lexicon that accompanies this bookless message, promulgated in education by technocratic organisations like the OECD, which has informed those modernising curriculums, most notably in Scotland, Wales and New Zealand, that include phrases like 'critical thinking', 'global competence' and 'emotional skills'. These are not real-world attributes. They are guesses made by individuals enamoured of innovation and entrepreneurialism. I was invited to speak at a Becta conference on innovation because of a software tool I'd designed, not long after I left the classroom. The keynote speech was by a Canadian innovation guru, and when the time came, I asked a simple question: 'Do you think innovation is always good?' He was visibly puzzled, and struggled to respond because it was obvious the question had never once occurred to him – something confirmed when he managed to reply hesitantly, 'I guess so. I've never thought about it.' One of my previous employers ran an internal Entrepreneur of the Year competition and received over 60 entries across the entire group. After months of judging, my team of three won. There was nothing especially entrepreneurial about what we did. I modified an idea for some software I'd seen used at the Karolinska Institute in Stockholm, recruited a talented sales colleague and technician I'd worked with before, and we dutifully jumped through every hurdle the company's senior management placed in front of us. That's how the real world works. Scientific and cultural problems aren't solved by party political deadheads, journalists or celebrities. They are solved by people with know-how, academic scholars, people who dedicate themselves to understanding their chosen field of study. US scientists weren't able to reproduce the coronavirus three hours after they had received the DNA sequence from the Chinese government because they were innovative or entrepreneurial; it was because they already had the knowledge it required. The essential attribute required is the same whether your specialism is electron microscopy or Keats. You literally need to *know* what you're talking about and what to do with it. That innocuous, clever little noun 'know-how' puts a lot of otherwise turgid talk about curriculum development into perspective.

Central to reading for every literature teacher is the part played by a library. Unusually, my various roles have taken me into some extraordinarily polarised schools. I've worked in fiercely selective private schools and inner-city schools that lack all three of the basic conditions for success I referred to earlier. A school I taught in for many years had a library most small towns would envy, with a view of St Paul's Cathedral and over the River Thames people pay millions for, while others have abandoned the idea altogether in favour of technology and have even renamed these vital educational tools 'learning centres' or something equally vapid. Many secondary schools I've seen allow a strange kind of hybrid to develop by default rather than design, and these libraries are often in effect just spaces with books used as timetable dumping grounds, polluted by IT. If the goal is the creation of readers who can successfully surrender themselves to someone else's thought through their prose – children who are in practice able to sit alone with a book and immerse themselves in it for extended periods of time – then a good library is a necessity, if not in school, then somewhere. Ideally, from the literature teacher's viewpoint, the secondary school library should be a place they know holds the range of texts, historically and generically, they need to support what they teach in the classroom. The minimum it needs to do is reflect and support your linguistic and literary timelines. It's no use being passionate about Shakespeare if the pupils you inspire aren't able to go to a library alone and find accessible copies of more plays to read. Similarly, they must know the conditions they find there meet their practical needs as readers. There's a reason all serious libraries are silent. School libraries are no different. It's something of a worrying responsibility, but every English department in a secondary school should be a dominant stakeholder in the school's library. They should concern themselves professionally with how it is managed and run.

Building their literary toolkit

Keeping firmly within the secondary school, real-world parameters I've set myself, what then are the literary tools pupils should be taught how to use?

Reading for aesthetic pleasure is an absolute prerequisite. You can never faithfully assess someone else's writing, appreciate why it has won the admiration of scholars and teachers (often generations of them before you) if you can't surrender yourself to the narrative of a fiction, sense the beauty of someone's verse or admire their stagecraft. That caricature member of the public who unashamedly admits they know nothing about art (but 'I know what I like') is someone who was never given a toolset. As I've stressed before and no doubt will do again, it's not good enough to assume these things will happen. You have to spell them out to your pupils. You have to actually tell them, repeatedly, what you want them to learn how to do. It's easy for English teachers, who are usually steeped in literature and books, to forget, as the faces change and the bodies get taller from one lesson to another, that even when you are teaching sixth formers, all your pupils are just putting their toes in literary waters in exactly the same way they are starting out on life. Neuroscientists like Sarah-Jayne Blakemore at UCL have challenged the lazy, legalistic idea that 18 is some kind of useful maturity threshold. Adolescence is above all that period when people construct a sense of themselves, and in the essentially social way that we think of it, it extends well into people's twenties. Teachers increasingly appreciate how important vocabulary and wider cultural knowledge are to successful reading, yet do they really appreciate how important the sheer volume of fiction that you read might be? Is reading *Great Expectations* when you have read less than a handful of complete novels even remotely like rereading it when you have read all of Charles Dickens, George Eliot, Thomas Hardy, Elizabeth Gaskell and Anthony Trollope? It's easy to forget you're always dealing with novices.

Those additional theatre or cinema trips can go a long way to nurturing these goals of wider reading and cultural experience but come with a small degree of risk. I can remember one occasion after a trip to see a David Lynch film, apologising to the pupils I'd inflicted it on. Shakespeare is especially vulnerable to cranks and agitprop evangelists. When the curtain goes up on *Macbeth* and the witches are on roller skates or wearing pastel pink tutus, you might find you have some explaining to do. Any 16-year-old who witnessed Peter O'Toole playing Macbeth in the '80s probably never set foot in a theatre again. Timothy West, artistic director of the Old Vic at the time, famously disowned it, and having witnessed it (it was, after all, a crime of sorts) I could see why. (The film director Josef von Sternberg, disowning his 1952 film *Macao*, said, 'Instead of fingers in that pie, half a dozen clowns immersed various parts of their anatomy in it.' By common agreement, there was only one digit in O'Toole's pie; it was just the size of a rolling pin.)

Reading a literary work with the confident expectation that you will learn something is equally important. Pupils need to be told this is another prime reason why the literature curriculum introduces them to great works and canonical writers. They should learn to value the opportunity to meet some of the world's most significant thinkers in the pages of their writing. C.S. Lewis wrote, 'Literature adds to reality, it does not simply describe it. It enriches the necessary competencies that daily life requires and provides; and in this respect, it irrigates the deserts that our lives have already become.' Pupils need to know he was serious, just as Stendhal was when he expressed this necessity more succinctly in his magnificent novel *Scarlet and Black*: 'A good book is an event in my life.' In *Areopagitica*, Milton of course argued, 'as good almost kill a Man as kill a good Book; who kills a Man kills a reasonable creature, Gods Image; but hee who destroyes a good Booke, kills reason it selfe, kills the Image of God, as it were in the eye.' These are arguments all students of literature need to know.

They also need to accept a further difficult responsibility. Studying literature often requires them to focus on one or more aspects of a writer's work, yet they have to learn how to assimilate the whole work before they can comment thoughtfully or valuably on any single aspect of it. There is always therefore a practical sequential aspect to literary scholarship. That first complete experience of the work of literature – whether it's a haiku, a Katherine Mansfield short story or Milton's *Paradise Lost* – is inevitably followed by a closer, different type of reading experience, one which demands you maintain a grip of the artistic whole, even while you interrogate separate, constituent parts of it as small as an individual phrase or word. When the text is poetry, that unit of attention shrinks even further and pupils need to learn how to identify and describe individual sounds and, more importantly, their intimate and often almost invisible relationship to one another. Poetry, more than any other form of textual study, demands you work with a magnifying glass.

In essence, when rereading like this, you have to learn to constantly question all the choices a writer makes. Why this word and not that? What does this image make the reader feel or think? How does the author steer your likes or dislikes? As with any toolset, some are used more frequently than others and pupils need to learn when and how to address one subsuming question because it lies at the heart of everything they are required to do at school. Whatever the object of study, however small the unit of attention or sweeping the narrative perspective, at some point they will need to ask themselves, 'How successful is this?'

They need to be taught what to expect and what to look out for, which is where teachers run a major risk of deskilling them. It's easy, when your time is largely consumed teaching lesson after lesson, day after day, to fall into the temptation to categorise and list. Lists are useful tools, like gauges. They tell pupils what to look out for but at the same time can narrow their vision. The only value in recognising and naming any technical feature of an author's work is that it gives you a basis from which to evaluate it. When you know and are historically and culturally familiar with what you're dealing with, you are less likely to misunderstand its use. Reading Seneca makes Jacobean drama appear far less grotesque. There's always a balance to be struck between efficiently teaching pupils new labels so that they can speak confidently about rhythm when they hear it on a page, or about tone and imagery; but knowing the difference between a metaphor and a metonym isn't an end in itself. No teacher's timetable is generous enough to accommodate covering the lengthy list of literary devices they could compile if they wanted to. A literary device may be a tool you can teach pupils how to use themselves, if what you are teaching them to do is to write fiction or verse; but when you're teaching them to become a skilful student of literature, it's only another piece of the jigsaw. It allows them to put the full picture together more quickly and accurately. Most teachers already do this, but (I suspect as a consequence of the conventional way texts are discussed and scrutinised) it happens live, in lessons. How they enhance their knowledge of technique and begin building an extensive, critical vocabulary of their own as part of their toolkit is a different matter I'll return to shortly.

Earlier, I pointed out how few complete literary texts secondary school pupils are realistically able to refer to as readers. It's inevitable, as they move up through a school and are taught specifically about literature, that they learn to evaluate what they read, which inevitably includes how to compare. An English curriculum embracing literature will put increasingly sophisticated texts in front of pupils as they age and their reading experience develops. In the real world, when only 30% of children between 8 and 18 say they read every day,[64] delivering this is a huge challenge. According to the OECD PISA tests in 2018, nearly half (48%) of 15-year-olds in England said they did not read for enjoyment, while

---

64. See above, p.67.

the average across all countries was 42%. More worryingly, a paltry 26% of English 15-year-olds reported reading for more than half an hour per day for pleasure, compared with 34% across the OECD.

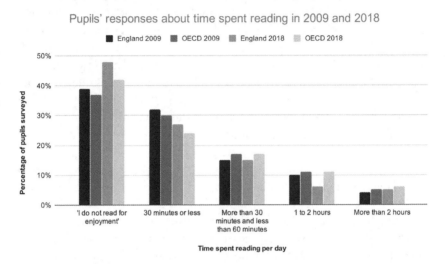

Figure 4 Reproduced by permission of the OECD, 2019. Data from www.bit.ly/ 39Dlfj4, accessed 11th January 2020.

Reacting to this by arguing that they need texts which are more 'relevant' or by asking them to study Shakespeare from a comic turns English teachers into conscientious objectors. It's simply abandoning the task as too difficult. The tool you want them to own is that ability to evaluate, which is simply impossible unless they can compare. Evaluation is really another way of saying they must demonstrate judgement; and the narrower one's frame of reference, the less credible one's judgement. In most UK schools, children won't opt to study literature; it will come with the territory if your teachers expect you to do reasonably well in your English at GCSE. Some schools may allow the pupil to choose, but either way, they must make it clear it's impossible to learn how to evaluate if all you commit to reading are the set texts. Reading needs to expand in line with their other skills. The first tool I said all literature pupils needed was the ability to read for aesthetic pleasure. They should know, in studying literature, they are signing up to a steadily increasing necessity to do just this.

As they learn to identify technique at work in a text, so they need to develop and use a literary vocabulary of their own. Part of this process means appreciating that some words are transferable across genres – 'character', 'tone', 'syntax' – while others aren't. At some point, their literary vocabulary needs to be subdivided by genre so there are terms they know to use when studying poetry – such as 'assonance', 'couplet' or 'caesura' – which don't apply to fiction. One of the step changes any experienced teacher will recognise in someone they've taught for a lengthy period is the point at which they exhibit this ability to use the right tool for the right job. The otherwise polished surfaces of innumerable answers in literature exams are scratched and damaged by pupils trying to use the wrong tool. They forget that plays have audiences, not readers, that rhyme is something you hear, or that scenes are not units in a novel. The lesson that genres have vocabularies peculiar to them should be taught, not learned by accident. However, it's a mistake to think this is purely an instructive exercise. Pupils also have to learn to be comfortable using this vocabulary. Far too many pupils pick up a literary vocabulary as labels only when they need to use them in the same, natural way they would choose other descriptive terms in conversation. This signals how important conversation and discussion are in the literature classroom. Good teachers know this too, of course, and a sign of a skilful literature teacher is how adept they are at stimulating and maintaining live discussion that requires high levels of participation by individuals. I recently came across a Twitter thread in which full-time teachers were discussing questioning techniques and was genuinely puzzled to see an exchange about the frequency of asking named individuals questions. I can think of only two reasons to begin a question in a lesson about literature with someone's name. The first is to engage them in a discussion they have been neglecting; and the second, to elicit their opinion. Otherwise, every question should be an open invitation.

In the same way they must possess a critical vocabulary subdivided by genre, they must learn how to modify the tools they use to suit the genre. One of the characteristics that distinguishes a skilful pupil from a moderate one is the confident way they think and write about different genres. When reading a play, they know to think in terms of the stage; when reading poetry, they think primarily about sound; and when reading fiction, they have little difficulty engaging their imagination in a narrative, however distant from their lived experience.

The development of this personal toolset must reflect what they are taught about each of the major literary genres – fiction, poetry and drama. Again, I think it's too easy for teachers to assume these three key terms are easily understood. They should be taught not (as many want teachers to do) as invitations or prompts to write creatively, but as conventions and formats to recognise instantly. Literary scholars are perfectly aware that what they are often describing when they study an author's work closely is the degree to which they break the rules or create new ones. Literature so often rises to the surface of cultural attention not by inherent beauty or original genius, but by contrast with what has gone before. But you have to *know* the rules before you can break them. Which is why teaching them is absolutely fundamental work at this stage in secondary school. Any child who has spent two or three years studying literature in secondary school should have no difficulty distinguishing prose from poetry or from drama, merely by its layout on the page. How often instead do 16-year-olds exhibit real doubt about what type of text they're dealing with while studying for GCSE? Picking out verse from prose in a Shakespeare play shouldn't be the intimidating task it undoubtedly is for many pupils.

In my preface, I made the point that if I were to return to the English classroom today, after everything I've learned since leaving it, I would have to do the job very differently. One of the most obvious new responsibilities literature teachers have to accept is the job of teaching pupils how to use technology to look for information. I don't see this as an especially technical exercise. I've worked with some very sophisticated technologies and for technology businesses long enough to have an informed perspective. Ever since computer sales staff first set foot in schools, alchemy has been their default sales strategy. Make sure the people you're talking to believe the magic. In 20 years, all that's changed are the incantations. The underlying strategy remains the same. You need only look at the way two little letters, 'A' and 'I', are deployed in a whole host of commercial contexts, picked up and naively replicated by the media, to see how it works. We're not actually interested in trying to explain to you what this particular algorithm does. In fact, because it's been built on top of a whole series of other hugely complex, automated calculations, we're not sure we even know ourselves, but trust us, it's *artificial* and it's *intelligent*. Busy politicians lap it up. Ofqual – the government department that regulates all school qualifications, exams and tests in England – is currently running an 'AI' initiative to see if software can mark English Language GCSE questions as accurately as the most experienced human markers.[65] One thing I quickly learned working with technology, particularly things in development, was just how stupid machines really are. (I suppose there's a logic to this. If you can only think in terms of a series of ones and noughts, what chance have you got against something that has 26 characters to play with?) One major project I worked on required us partnering with a specialist security business, and it was so refreshing to hear them in every discussion talk about people. Even though, in layman's terms, they sold some of the most advanced software systems imaginable, they knew (and stressed to all their customers) that computer security is always a human problem. The wisest thing Ofqual could do is replace all references to 'AI' with 'AA' because there will be nothing intelligent about the process whatsoever: all the machines will be doing is automated assessment.

This helps explain why teaching students of literature how to use internet search engines is essentially a discussion about academic and scholarly provenance. Instead of worrying about internet search protocols, literature students need to know *where* to look more than *how*. I learned this lesson while I was actually still teaching when what initially looked like a useful US website dedicated to *Macbeth* started to throw up some curious ideas about the play and some even more quirky links. A little bit of rooting around and I realised the entire resource had been created by the National Rifle Association. A secondary school literature teacher these days must be something of an expert in online provenance. They should have favourite digital collections, libraries, individual scholars and archives they know they can rely on for credible information. And just because someone claims expertise online doesn't mean they possess anything other than a keyboard and an ego.

One of the most useful and rapid-return things you can teach using technology is how to research an author's life and work. However long or short the text, whoever the author, there comes a point in every literary study when learning something about the person behind the pen

---

65. www.bit.ly/3aNQGbX, accessed 10th January 2020.

becomes useful knowledge. Biography as a distinct nonfiction format is something that can be looked at in English lessons and increasingly is, but when studying literature in secondary school, there are substantial gains to be made not by adding Lucy Worsley's insightful biography of Jane Austen or Claire Tomalin's *Charles Dickens: A Life* to their reading list but just by pointing them in the direction of an authoritative online resource. A website like *Luminarium* or *The Victorian Web* has succinct biographical material that is invaluable when, as a teenager, you are trying to fit a writer and their work into your personal literary schema. Knowing even a little of an author's personal history rarely fails to illuminate your understanding of their work. More pertinently, knowing absolutely nothing about them – the historical period in which they lived and wrote, the wider culture out of which their work rose to significance – is the cause of multiple errors in literary essays. This specific ignorance somehow frequently finds its way into the GCSE exam room; and in real-world English terms, it's simply unforgivable.

Every pupil studying literature should be taught how to quickly and efficiently locate an author's key biographical details online as a scholarly, not technical, exercise in which provenance is what matters. In any employment where I have had a technology sales responsibility, I always take the view that, as an educational consultant, my job is to understand the educational value any given technology really offers. When *Wikipedia* first appeared, I was working for an employer who was quick to encourage the use of 'wikis' by teachers. This was shortly after I had published my book on John Donne, so I had a look at *Wikipedia* and the entry on Donne. To say it was peremptory would be overselling it. There were a few brief paragraphs, mostly wrong, and *Wikipedia* had flagged it as a page which needed improvement, so I added some key biographical details. I then kept an eye on it over the following months. It wasn't long before I started seeing things I'd written deleted or altered, and at first I diligently amended these; but when I started seeing how often someone (who was almost certainly just a US high school student) was adding nonsensical material about Donne's attitude to love or to women, I abandoned the project as hopeless. All these years later, the *Wikipedia* entry on Donne is now lengthy and mostly factually accurate but reads like notes hastily taken down by a high school student in a class taught by someone whose knowledge of Donne is drawn from various children's encyclopaedias. I still treat *Wikipedia* with immense caution.

Technology also provides opportunities to study literature through audio or video resources that were simply not around two decades ago. Provenance matters here too, and what pupils need are recommendations more than vague encouragements to explore. Given the marginal role theatre plays in contemporary culture, it's a safe bet most secondary school pupils will have never seen a Shakespearean play performed live in a theatre. A theatre audience that thinks it's a sensible procedure to use their mobile phones to capture clips of their favourite celebrity is wasting their ticket money. Somehow, real-world English teachers have to navigate these extremes so that pupils know how to enjoy a stage play, if that's what they choose to do in the future, and how to use a different production format, like film or TV, to support their study of what is always, in essence, a play script. There is a logical process to think about teaching Shakespeare that makes sensible use of real-world conditions. Pupils have a right to experience Shakespeare in a theatre if at all possible. Whether at the RSC in Stratford-upon-Avon, the Globe in London, or other regional theatres when opportunities arise, ideally any child studying *Macbeth*, *Romeo and Juliet* or *Julius Caesar* should have the chance to simply experience it as it was intended, as a theatrical delight and a pleasure. There is absolutely no need for them to know anything about the play before they take their seat. The media narrative that positions Shakespeare as the English equivalent of quadratic equations is unhelpful as well as absurd. But it also illustrates how lacking in sequential thinking the English curriculum has been for decades. No child who had learned a timeline to the English language, and who had the kind of linguistic and etymological experience I outlined in chapter two, would regard Shakespeare's verse as a foreign language, which is of course the common complaint. They would understand how language changes over time and be prepared to see unfamiliar words and familiar words being used differently. If you were to take a speech from any of these three plays – say Romeo's speech under the balcony or Mark Antony's speech at Caesar's funeral – and put it in front of a class, the likelihood is that the difficulty narrative has been so well imbibed, they will genuinely struggle. If instead, you took the same speech, simply reproduced it as a jumbled list of single words, and asked them to pick out all those they didn't understand, most would find only one or two words they didn't recognise; and if you suggested it wasn't English, they would think you mad. Imagine if you asked them next to use any of those words to form new sentences. Would they struggle? So often, English teachers are having to fight against wider cultural messages they need to recognise and defuse before they counter them. If 'the best that has been thought and said' doesn't include William Shakespeare, what are you going to teach them?

I learned early in my teaching career to avoid the special performances put on by professional theatres for schools if at all possible, and to take smaller groups to evening performances where the adults outnumbered them. This neutralises much of the social distraction that inevitably happens when large numbers of teenagers from different schools fill any space. I used to be able to walk a class to the Globe Theatre (and can only imagine how many English teachers would give their right arm to do the same), but that in itself is not without its problems. In an afternoon schools' production of *Julius Caesar*, actors playing various commoners addressed by the tribunes Flavius and Murullus were stationed amongst the groundling audience at the Globe. They went unnoticed by a group of teenagers, gleefully socialising, who were standing in front of me. As the play was about to start, this group showed no sign of interest in anything other than each other and started to drop their empty drinks cans on the ground and stamp on them. The volume of noise this game produced was considerable, but it came to an abrupt end when an actor, dressed as a commoner, swung round to face them and yelled as only a Shakespearean actor can, 'Will you shut the f*** up!' The effect was, in all senses, dramatic, and two of the girls scuttled to the side of their teacher, who happened to be standing close to me, to complain in whispers about that 'horrible man'. An English teacher who doesn't understand that they will need to teach some teenagers how to behave at the theatre is only doing half the job.

If, as will often be the case, you have no opportunity to see a stage version before any page is turned or iambic pentameter uttered or stuttered in the classroom, you should give pupils the chance to enjoy the play in a different format. Part of the job is to know which film or TV version to choose because there's no shortage and some are better than others. Do this successfully and there's no reason why most pupils will not have a complete narrative fixed in their memory before they start to read anything. That is in itself a huge advantage and means you all have something to reference in lessons that will inevitably focus on the text. The same sequence applies to any play, ancient or modern, with the only proviso that any dramatist other than Shakespeare is likely to be less well served on film or TV.

The same principle applies to all poetry. Pupils should be given the chance to listen to it first, before ever interrogating any words on the page. The great advantage here is that you don't need a professional actor to read poetry aloud. I used to teach *The Rime of the Ancient Mariner* and discovered I could read the entire poem in one lesson. Lots of poetry is available in audio format, especially online, but again the teacher's job is advisory and often about provenance. I've listened to a lot of poetry, live and recorded, and there are two key things to watch out for. Just because someone wrote a poem doesn't mean they can read it. This weakness has no respect for name, awards or reputation. Never assume that a reading by a famous poet of their own verse will be useful. Actors, people who make a living out of speaking clearly and aloud, tend to make much better readers of verse than amateurs. I listened to quite a few audio versions of *Paradise Lost* when I wrote my guidebook to Milton's epic, and although there are some really useful amateur readings downloadable online (the University of Cambridge's English Faculty's, for example), the professional ones tend to outshine them. BBC Radio 4 produced a version in 2010 (which is still available online) in which the actor Ian McDiarmid played Satan. It exemplifies just how much skilled professional readers can do to enhance a student's experience and understanding of difficult verse. It makes no sense in the real world to expect students to silently read Milton's epic when they can first of all listen to someone as skilled as McDiarmid taking them to hell and back.

The second key thing to avoid is in itself a truly bizarre literary phenomenon. Far too many people, even some successful poets, have developed this curious idea that when you read a poem, you must adopt a completely different, unnatural, druidical voice. This new voice must sound both portentous and monotonous, while simultaneously being mind-numbingly dull to listen to. If the poem has different character voices within it, you must ignore them. If it contains words or phrases that even in isolation sound beautiful, they must be suffocated before they can raise a smile or stir a tear. Sometimes it comes with its own unearthly form of vibrato. Sadly, I have even heard teachers use this voice. It is the kiss of death to real poetry. I suspect it's a result of that tendency you find all too often in poetic circles to form a clique. Somehow, the phenomenal memory and presumably beautiful voice of the communal, Homeric rhapsode gave way over centuries to the romantic, often Bohemian individual, whose tortured soul needed a tortured voice. It's a cliché we still struggle to shake off. The line-up of speakers at any modern poetry event today looks like a cross between a Victorian criminologist's scrapbook and a cutting-edge hair stylists' convention.

As children progress in their literary studies, they should also be taught how to use audio and video resources independently to support their own reading. In the real world, there is an oversupply of literature teachers, even though many schools would find that a particularly bitter pill to swallow. New technologies have encouraged many literary scholars to record what they do in the lecture theatre and make it widely available. Although much of this kind of material is university level, many scholars have a public profile that means they pitch some of their work to a general audience, and this is often extremely useful material for secondary school literature students. It's far better for them that their teacher points them in the right direction than they waste valuable time guessing and searching. The real-world teacher of literature shouldn't be afraid to exploit the wealth of scholarly material that spills over from formal publications.

There is one final skill that's easily overlooked by English teachers because it's assumed every child will simply pick it up. They need to learn how to use a keyboard as well as a pen. This doesn't imply the demise of the handwritten exam. Technology advocates have been pushing this criminal idea for decades now. They mock the fact that in the '21st century', children still write their answers by hand, and that schools don't allow them to use all the creative software available to them to… be creative. It's doubly damaging. It makes the mistake of reducing handwriting to nothing more than a practical skill when it should be considered an essential educational right, as potent and fundamental as reading. It conveniently ignores the inevitable and profoundly worrying consequence that, over time, as handwriting falls into disuse in schools, generations will lose the ability to represent what they think without the aid of a keyboard. Predictive text is the thin edge of a dangerously obese wedge.

Literature matters in the real world

That's quite a large toolbox, but the nature of teaching being what it is, I've no doubt professional teachers will be more than able to add some of their own. What I've tried to do is focus on what might be considered the essentials, in the same way that it's essential an English curriculum covers those three major genres – fiction, poetry and drama. But there's another educational imperative to introducing children to these three. A lot has been written in recent years – ever since a previous UK Education Secretary, Michael Gove, quoted Matthew Arnold's essay *Culture and Anarchy,* in arguing schools should teach 'the best that has been thought and said'. It's worth making the point clearly that Arnold (besides being an inspector of schools and son of Thomas Arnold, the headmaster of Rugby School) was himself a poet and a professor of poetry at Oxford. He was steeped in educational purpose and practice. Most recently, the debate has focused on the concept of 'cultural capital' popularised by French sociologist Pierre Bourdieu. It's a clumsy piece of Marxist borrowing, something Bourdieu himself even acknowledged because he thought 'informational capital' captured the idea better. But if you need a French sociologist to tell you knowing important stuff is really 'cultural capital', you have an educational problem, not a linguistic one.

There are numerous teachers and school leaders working hard today on bridging what they perceive as a cultural deficit faced by many of the children they teach. If your parents talked to you, played with you, took you to see interesting things in interesting places, and read to you every evening at bedtime, the chances are starting school will be both exciting and purposeful. If you had none of these advantages, it won't – not least because you'll walk into the building with several thousand fewer words in your head than your more fortunate chums. In 2018, the Oxford Language Report *Why Closing the Vocabulary Gap Matters* surveyed 473 primary and 840 secondary teachers; 'over half of those surveyed reported that at least 40% of their pupils lacked the vocabulary to access their learning. 69% of primary school teachers and over 60% of secondary school teachers believe the word gap is increasing.'[66]

66. www.bit.ly/344GQzx, accessed 30th January.

Whatever you like to call it, some children start school ready for it; others don't. This is a parenting problem, but expecting contemporary politicians to address anything to do with parenting or the family is like asking a vegan to lend a hand in an abattoir. So the problem is a school's problem, at least for the foreseeable future. It persists in secondary school, and teachers of literature in particular have a lot of ground to make up. When I worked as a tutor for Teach First, supporting some two dozen trainees in London secondary schools, one of my tutees' most common observations was surprise at realising how geographically restricted the lives of those they taught were. These were, at the time, some of the UK's top graduates, with good degrees from leading Russell Group universities and a cultural and personal pedigree to match. If you've been skiing every winter since you were six and your own teachers had taken you to Pompeii, Berlin or Beijing, it was a genuine shock to discover most of those sitting in front of you had never even strayed beyond a three-mile radius from their home. A literature teacher introducing children to drama as a genre is almost certainly going to be talking to a majority of pupils who have never set foot in a theatre, except possibly for a Christmas pantomime or, at best, a musical. If you go to see a stage play today in London that isn't on any GCSE or A level syllabus, the average age of the audience is deceased. This is quite a responsibility if you take Arnold's injunction seriously. Theatre might be a lifeless, shrivelled corpse of a thing today, kept alive only by big tunes and small politics, but that's not always been the case, and part of the job is to make sure they know that.

As an English teacher, I felt it was my responsibility to give those I taught every opportunity I could to experience great drama and cinema. In my first term in the job, I received an invitation from a local university cinema to an exclusive schools' screening of Roman Polanski's *Tess* that included nibbles and wine afterwards. I sorted out a minibus enthusiastically and sent off for the tickets. A few weeks later, I received a polite letter telling me they had had to cancel because, out of 86 schools they had mailed written invitations to, I was the only one to reply. It was one of those career-defining lessons most teachers can point to. Encouraged by my youngest daughter, I recently did a huge clear-out in my garage and discovered a box in which I had stored all the theatre programmes I had accumulated over my years as an English teacher. I used to keep them on the surface of a cupboard in my classroom for pupils to use as reference material. There were exactly 100, including one from the Bolshoi Theatre and others from France, Germany, Canada and the USA. One memory in particular feels apposite. Watching a production of *The Glass Menagerie* at the Royal Exchange Theatre in Manchester, from my seat I could see all of the pupils I'd taken sitting along a row to my right. The staging included a series of glass shelves covered with the miniature glass figurines that formed the menagerie. As visible trickles of water ran down the menagerie after the glass unicorn had been broken, one of the most subtle, cleverest bits of technical theatre I've ever seen, I noticed one of my least literary, most reluctant pupils was trying, and failing, to hold back his own tears. This isn't something you can examine, but it matters just as much as the things you can.

In arguing that literature teaching in secondary schools must encompass a far-reaching, historical perspective, I'm aware that some will be quick to raise a very fashionable contemporary objection. The argument, as I understand it, regards Western literature as a woefully unbalanced litany from the pens of a lot of dead white European males. This is historically accurate. It took a combination of effective gynaecology and contraception to loosen the intimate bonds that bound women to their homes and families ever since homes have been on their shopping list, but so what? History, unlike shopping, isn't negotiable. Literature deals in significant ideas and such ideas don't quiver or fall, however fiercely identarian one's gaze. Subjecting the study of literature to either a racial or sexual filter is a self-deluding lie, nothing more.

The decolonisation of literature is a trite, entirely politically motivated cause that regards knowledge as an opportunity cost worth paying by others for what it perceives as the greater political good. Teenagers have a right to know literary truth just as they have a right to be taught the fundamental laws of physics or the properties of a triangle. You study the history of literature to know what was written and by whom, not what your teacher would have preferred to have been written. If you think, like a detectorist, the field is bursting with hidden, unknown gems, you will be just as routinely disappointed because previous readers and scholars have already decided what is and what is not durable. Unlike a detectorist, you won't be uncovering anything, just rewriting history to suit your own ephemeral place in it. Decolonisers deceive only themselves when they assert that their mission is all about balance.

So why does any of this matter in the real world – a world I have acknowledged is replete with technologies that affect every imaginable aspect of teaching literature? In the end, we teach literature because the knowledge it conveys is every bit as powerful as the knowledge conveyed by empirical science. No matter how ubiquitous the hardware or 'intelligent' the software, human beings don't speak to each other in a blinding stream of ones and noughts.

CHAPTER FOUR
REAL-WORLD TECHNOLOGY

There's no avoiding technology

In the preface, I related how I had left teaching in the classroom, largely because I thought technology was going to change the way people taught and I had no desire to be on the receiving end. I was absolutely right in predicting change; I just had no idea how dramatic it would be. Before I ever entered a classroom as a teacher, I was handed my master's degree in English by a winner of the Nobel Prize in Literature. I never forgot something he said in his address. All the degrees being awarded that day were arts degrees and he had quite a simple message that is as powerfully pertinent today as it was then. He said, 'Whenever anyone doubts the value of an arts degree, remember you're the people who make sure the scientists don't change the world for the worse.' This was over a decade before the internet became publicly available, yet how wonderfully prescient the author of *The Spire* and *Lord of the Flies* proved to be. Politicians internationally are currently floundering around looking for ways to unpick the damage that unbridled, fast-moving technological innovation has inflicted on our culture. Female journalists complain that dating apps have rendered the entire experience of falling in love a misery. Study after study finds children dedicating more hours to their screens than to actually living. One false step online can see the shares in any business plummet. It turns out Orwell's telescreen is called Alexa.

Technology has become so pervasive and persuasive, it challenges not just how people teach, but what they teach and why. Even more profoundly, it has reached the stage where it mediates almost every aspect of how we communicate using English. Apart from face-to-face conversation, there is almost no communicative act that doesn't now involve choice – often multiple choices because the range of devices and software applications those devices offer us is so wide. Even the relatively simple act of writing a book using a laptop means you are bombarded with choice. The machine I'm using to write this offers me a choice of 388 different fonts...I counted. The standard menu bar I'm using contains 45 different 'buttons', many of those inviting much wider choice the moment I click on them. Even relatively simple apps on mobile phones entice you to choose all the time. They can't even provide you with predictive text without urging you to choose this word instead of another. In chapter one, I pointed out how this choice affects something as conventionally neutral as an educational research paper, and the creators end up publishing something wholly different to a black and white sheet, from which the text is allowed to speak for itself. Technology all too often generates marketing colour and practice where it isn't needed. Anyone who uses presentation software like PowerPoint or Keynote will know the feeling of being faced with a plethora of choices you'd prefer not to have to make. Like it or not, English teachers today must grasp the profound educational implications of all this if they are to prepare pupils for the real world. Thinking openly about the relationship between technology and the written word is not an optional extra. English teachers need to be as critically aware of the relationship between something written and the technology employed in its production as they commonly are about the intricacies of the language itself.

Turn the tables

Not long after I'd left the profession, the call for teachers to use technology in their classroom became deafening and it's barely abated. What English teachers should be doing is turning the tables. Today, instead of worrying about whether or not they use technology in the classroom, English teachers should be unequivocally chorusing James Williams's demand: *Stand Out of Our Light.*[67] Williams explains in admirable detail how these technologies are all in the business of demanding our attention. 'What *do* you pay when you pay attention? You pay with all the things you could have attended to, but didn't: all the goals you didn't pursue, all the actions you didn't take, and all the possible yous you could have been, had you attended

---

67. See above, p. 11.

to those other things.'[68] His book is an inspiring rallying call to anyone who has ever felt technology is not working in their best interests. Towards its close, Williams articulates the change we all need to make in an impassioned rallying call. English teachers, like it or not, are in the vanguard:

> We have to demand that these forces to which our attention is now subject start standing out of our light. This means rejecting the present regime of attentional serfdom. It means rejecting the idea that we're powerless, that our angry impulses must control us, that our suffering must define us, or that we ought to wallow in guilt for having let things get this bad. It means rejecting novelty for novelty's sake and disruption for disruption's sake. It means rejecting lethargy, fatalism, and narratives of us versus them … Future generations will judge us not only for our stewardship of the outer environment, but of the inner environment as well. Our current crisis does not only come in the form of rising global temperatures, but also in our injured capacities of attention. Our mission, then, is not only to reengineer the world of matter, but also to reengineer our world so that we can give attention to what matters.[69]

The impact of pervasive technology

It's worth starting this argument with the big hitters. In June 2018, the RAND Corporation delivered its lengthy evaluation of the Gates Foundation's Effective Teacher initiative, a $212 million investment between 2009 and 2016. The financial cost to participating schools was even more, some $575 million. RAND concluded that 'the initiative did not achieve its goals for student achievement or graduation, particularly for LIM (low income minority) students'.[70] Others who studied their report

68. Williams, James, (2018). *Stand Out of Our Light*, Cambridge University Press, p. 45.

69. Ibid, p.127.

70. Stecher, Brian M., Deborah J. Holtzman, Michael S. Garet, Laura S. Hamilton, John Engberg, Elizabeth D. Steiner, Abby Robyn, Matthew D. Baird, Italo A. Gutierrez, Evan D. Peet, Iliana Brodziak de los Reyes, Kaitlin Fronberg, Gabriel Weinberger, Gerald P. Hunter, and Jay Chambers, Improving Teaching Effectiveness: Final Report: The Intensive Partnerships for Effective Teaching Through 2015–2016. Santa Monica, CA: RAND Corporation, 2018. www. bit.ly/39J7YVX, accessed 12th January 2020.

thought they were on the generous side. Results didn't just fail categorically to achieve the project's goals; they were generally negative across a wide variety of outcomes. I suspect experienced teachers will find some of the report's recommendations genuinely amusing. The report suggested:

> A near-exclusive focus on TE might be insufficient to dramatically improve student outcomes. Many other factors might need to be addressed, ranging from early childhood education, to students' social and emotional competencies, to the school learning environment, to family support. Dramatic improvement in outcomes, particularly for LIM students, will likely require attention to many of these factors as well.

Unsurprisingly, data on teacher observations and pupil performance was the central (and decidedly shaky) pillar on which the project was built. No technology company I have ever worked for makes a decision, even about the biscuits, without consulting a spreadsheet. Data is their bread and butter, the blood that flows through their cables, so consequently they think it works the same way everywhere else too. Many educational researchers and policy makers in the UK make use of data from an organisation called FFT Education Datalab. They are part of a non-profit company called FFT Education and describe themselves as expert analysts of education data. I wonder how many of those researchers also know that the FFT stands for the Fischer Family Trust, a charity formed by successful entrepreneur Mike Fischer, cofounder and lifetime president of the largest educational technology group in the UK, RM. FFT Datalab is what you get when technologists are convinced everything they know and do will improve what schools know and do. Dataism, a faith in data to provide all the answers, is at its heart. Coined by the journalist David Brooks in an article for *The New York Times* in 2013, 'dataism' has been picked up by the widely read Israeli historian Yuval Noah Harari, who stresses the phenomenon's similarity with religious belief. Unfortunately for the faithful, all great schools are unique, which is the rock upon which most research and all randomised controlled trials in education inevitably flounder.

It's there in every attempt to use technology to improve or even 'transform' education, though they usually fall apart the moment anyone turns to the data for evidence of success because, as experienced teachers all know, teaching children is not an activity easily reduced to statistics, even red, amber or green ones. Educational 'transformation' was actually what companies bidding to supply technology into the lucrative BSF (Building Schools for the Future) market in England in the 2000s were asked to deliver. Quite a challenge, even considering the £1475 per pupil technology budget allocated to the programme by central government. Yet another example of how single words can have major real-world consequences.

There's a second recommendation RAND made which has significant real-world implications, not just for English teachers: 'Reformers should not underestimate the resistance that could arise if changes to teacher-evaluation systems have major negative consequences for staff employ-ment.' One of the things RAND believed happened was that school principals tended to rate teachers more highly than they should have done because they weren't especially happy giving negative evaluations and weren't convinced that weak staff would be removed. So over time, scores were inflated. Knowing teachers were likely to stay in post, they simply preferred to stay on good terms with them. A reminder that real people neither speak nor think in a stream of ones and noughts.

The threat to employment that technology poses is everywhere. The popular euphemism to describe this is 'disruption', as though losing one's job is ever a minor affair. The newspaper and publishing industries, entirely dependent on the written word, have been thrown in the air by technology and are taking years to settle. Live music, television and financial trading have all been turned inside out and an entirely new breed of Futurists has appeared who sell crystal ball gazing as consultancy. If you needed any more evidence about the insidious relationship between language and technology, look no further than a situation where the word to describe a new job title is widely adopted by businesses without anyone picking up a dictionary to see what a Futurist really is. Mussolini would have been thrilled.[71] Today's Futurists like painting a picture of a world where our old friend artificial intelligence has taken all the drudgery out of work. Any task that is repetitious, any role which is essentially formulaic or routine, will be passed on to a computer: 'Anything that

---

71. Filippo Tommaso Marinetti, the leading voice of the Italian Futurist movement wrote, 'We will glorify war – the world's only hygiene, militarism, patriotism, the destructive gesture of freedom-bringers, beautiful ideas worth dying for, and scorn for woman.'

can be automated, digitized or virtualized will be. This is as certain as music is in the cloud, cars are driving themselves, and money is going digital. Automation is reducing the need for rode [sic] and manual labor everywhere, and smart machines will soon do the knowledge work as well.'[72] It's that last assertion I want to focus on here because it's merely the latest incarnation of 'Why bother reading a book when you can google it?' It would be easy to assume I'm simply being neo-Luddite about this and deliberately underselling the benefits of technology. I'm not at all. I convinced my English colleagues to get an internet connection around 1995 before our school had one and when modems still made that weird, annoying, tinny sound. One reason I was seconded from my teaching role was because I won an award for a website I created. A broadband art tool I designed in 2000 turned up a decade later on Google. I can point to a healthy professional track record of using technology when I can see its advantages. I recall when I first came across a visualiser at BETT and thought just how invaluable it would be in a classroom and how much more useful and practical it was compared to any interactive whiteboard. Today, it's gratifying to see so many teachers use them and love them. But for every visualiser, there are dozens of interactive whiteboards. For every sensible, practical device or software application available to schools, there are dozens of useless red herrings some naive, techno zealot purse holder will buy for them. Working on a major consultancy project for a large group of schools involved me interviewing dozens of headteachers. One thing easily topped the anxiety list for almost all of them and it wasn't school inspection. It was technology. The reason being that they all knew it was the second largest item on their budget after staff salaries, but they also knew they were utterly clueless as to how to judge its educational value.

That Futurist guess that 'smart machines will soon do the knowledge work as well' has already been picked up by education businesses, lobbyists, policy makers and (most damagingly of all) naive politicians as an invitation to reduce the numbers of teachers in classrooms. You could decorate a school hall with white papers and research extolling the benefits of e-learning, online education and MOOCs, in spite of which schools remain an essential component of the education system and high-quality

---

72. Gerd Leonhard, www.bit.ly/346dwc9, accessed 12th February, 2020.

teachers a scarce resource. I suspect Jonathan Chocqueel-Mangan, director of strategy at Pearson, was right when he said at the FutureBook19 conference, 'We don't think technology is ever going to replace teachers.' However, that isn't going to be true for most current pupils. Technology is indeed primed to replace millions of those routine jobs worldwide in the near future, and if English teachers want to be preparing those they teach for that reality; they need to change what they're doing. The West has already seen a dramatic reduction in manual labour, especially in manufacturing, where machines perform excellently; and as I've already noted, the move into white collar roles has already begun. What better way could you prepare children for such an eventuality than by teaching them to be knowledgeable, confident users of the English language? If schools are serious about giving attention to what matters, the use of English would top my list.

Teachers who follow and participate in discussions about education and research will be very familiar with the way fads and trends sweep through schools. The list of edu-myths that have taken hold in schools, only to be ultimately exposed as groundless, is a long one – and depressing when you pause to reflect on how many children have had their brief spell in school warped and weakened as a result. How this happens is curious and in part a reflection of the lack of confidence within the teaching profession itself. A more confident profession would demand a far higher standard of credibility about anything that threatened the status quo than has been applied to so many recent innovations. The reality that we also have too many schools perceived as failing those they teach doesn't help. It makes it easier for external lobbyists, poorly qualified consultants, businesses and politicians to find fertile ground, even for the least sensible ideas. Far too many people forget that, as we discussed earlier, schools rely entirely for their success on three relatively simple propositions: knowledgeable, skilled teachers; supportive parents; and co-operative children. If policy makers and politicians would just concern themselves with providing these three things, schools would be far less vulnerable to fads and trends. One of the most widespread and debilitating myths relating to technology, which has had an impact on schools and teachers over decades now, is the idea that teenagers are 'digital natives'. The term was first coined by a US computer games designer, Marc Prensky, and rapidly adopted by business as a powerful marketing message. It's one of the most unpleasant strategies I've seen because it relied on undermining that crucial co-operative relationship. It set pupils and teachers in opposition to one another and required teachers to abandon their prime role as adults. Teachers were described as 'digital immigrants', naive newcomers, floundering around in a world where those they were teaching knew more than they did. It was educational claptrap, of course, nothing more than a clever and successful use of English for marketing purposes; but it hasn't quite disappeared. It lingers in discussions about whether or not technology is rewiring children's brains and all those transhumanist analogies that like to compare the human brain to a computer – analogies neuroscientists have no time for.

In a blog post titled, 'What can the PISA 2018 scores tell us about digital natives?', Daisy Christodoulou, the author of *Seven Myths about Education*, considered some of the implications of PISA introducing more computer-based reading tasks designed, as PISA believe, 'to make use of the affordances of computer-based testing and that reflect the new situations in which students apply their reading skills in real life'. They first attempted this in 2009, when researchers studying the results concluded, 'Most 15-year-old students do not know how to begin evaluating material they encounter on the internet. There is ample evidence that a majority of students consider it first in terms of relevance or interest, rather than looking at the reliability of its source.' New tests in 2018 produced a not dissimilar conclusion: 'Fewer than 1 in 10 students in OECD countries was able to distinguish between fact and opinion.'[73] As with everything to do with PISA, a lot of time could be spent interrogating the validity of the questioning. If the format of the question does not replicate exactly what 15-year-olds expect and experience when they go online, how credible is it? Reading material that doesn't use the precise design and layout its authors used when they published it online is hardly a valid test. Nonetheless, what is worth noting is that pupils did not find these reading tasks easy. If schools aren't teaching them to read online successfully, how well are they preparing them for the real world? This is why I placed such weight, earlier in chapter three, on teaching pupils about provenance, and it has implications for every English teacher. You can only do this when you take your own research skills and knowledge seriously and

---

73. www.bit.ly/39BAVDv, accessed 13th February 2020.

maintain a professional interest in archives, libraries and other significant online sources of useful material for those you teach. The explosion in material published online that social media has nurtured forces all of us to become our own editors. Some are better at it than others. Things we used to rely on as reasonable indicators of quality no longer apply, and it's not unusual to see articles published by national newspapers online which, had they been written by an A level or GCSE pupil, would require a skilled teacher's help. Blogging has generated a particular problem and is fraught with provenance and reliability issues. I recently saw a blog about teaching writing in high school which was itself sprinkled liberally with incorrect punctuation, poor word choice and genuine unintelligibility. Blogs are the Wild West of contemporary publishing.

Simultaneously, it's important to teach pupils about the risks of writing online. These are considerable yet little understood by many people who are active on social media. EduTwitter readers will be very aware of how personal, unpleasant and threatening some people become online. This is one of those areas where schools can learn a lot from good businesses. I've been in a meeting with a senior accountant from a business I worked for and found myself wishing I was near enough to kick them under the table as they repeatedly bad-mouthed the company we both worked for in front of a client. In contrast, I worked for huge business where, even on a Friday night in a bar after a hellish week, you would not find a single employee with a harsh word to say about their employer. The idea that you would ever criticise the business anywhere, in any shape or form, was unthinkable. Some schools could gain a lot from their example. This is all real-world English teaching. Children need to know what they face when they leave school and start to write online, just as they need to know what a metaphor is and who came first, Shakespeare or Shelley. How well do we currently teach pupils how to assess the risks or advantages of publishing personal opinions for the entire world to see? Is it in any curriculum or exam specification?

About 15 years ago, while working for a leading educational technology company, I started writing a blog because, as with most technologies my employer was asking people to buy, I wanted to know how it really worked before I discussed it with potential customers. As a senior educational employee, a key part of my role was to understand and articulate the educational values and benefits of the products and services the company sold. It didn't take me long to realise there were considerable professional risks to committing personal and educational opinions for public scrutiny. Even though I worked in educational technology, I never hid my scepticism or concerns in my blog and I was openly critical of techno zealots long before it became fashionable to challenge edtech. I publicised the work of US author Larry Cuban in the UK, whose book *Oversold and Underused: Computers in the Classroom* was one of the earliest alarm calls about the naive use of technology in schools.

Some years later, seeking a new role, I noticed a sudden spike in my blog readership. The same two IP addresses popped up all over the place with a particular individual's name being repeatedly searched for. After two interviews, my head-hunter was convinced I had secured the position; but then a curiously unexplained delay occurred, and I was asked back for a final 'conversation' with an ex-educator not employed by the new business, but who had a historical connection with the failing brand they had bought for a song, which the business wanted me to reinvent. After weeks of delay, frustration and confusion, I was not appointed. A few months later, the individual whose name had been repeatedly searched for on my blog, and who had a close relationship with the ex-educator who I realised had in effect vetoed my appointment, announced they had taken up the role. That they lasted a matter of months in a role they were entirely unsuited for was of little consolation. Shortly after that, I shut my blog down.

Although I was a professional author, I avoided Twitter for years because I shared the novelist Jonathan Franzen's view, in an interview he gave to *The Guardian* in 2012, that it was 'the ultimate irresponsible medium'.[74] In the end, I followed the advice of my publisher and succumbed to it a few years ago, but I still find it a difficult medium to manage, and have repeatedly advised my two undergraduate daughters to avoid it as they both have their entire careers before them. Anyone who uses it regularly will be aware of how often someone becomes the focus of intense, targeted anger. People quite rightly refer to this as 'mob' behaviour; it closely resembles the chaotic frenzy of blind emotion Dickens captured so well in *Barnaby Rudge*. It happened to me before I joined, and it's a measure of how powerful it is that I was acutely aware I was in the midst of a Twitter

---

74. www.bit.ly/39G2N9s, accessed 15th February, 2020.

storm, even though my virtual life excluded it. For having the temerity to suggest in my column for *Tes* that much young adult fiction had little literary merit and attracted more proselytizers than novelists (an opinion I think few would question today following the appearance of the term 'woke' and various scandals to hit the YA world),[75] I was pilloried online by thousands of people who knew nothing about me but were nonetheless prepared to attack me personally. I even had US librarians – people whose most aggressive act normally is to put a finger on their lips and say, 'Shhh!' – calling for me to lose my job. I ended up having to defend myself on the BBC's flagship radio news programme *Today*. I think subsequent events in that part of the publishing world have vindicated my view that most YA fiction is adolescents writing for other adolescents.

Both my blogging and Twitter experiences are informative examples of English in the real world. I don't think they are particularly exceptional. It must be part of every English department's role to prepare children for this kind of eventuality, not passed on to some external charity with their own agenda to deliver. They need to educate their pupils holistically not just about *how* to use the English language, but where, why and what the consequences may be. One of the worst side effects of schools being targeted by external organisations and individuals seeking to use them to further their own agenda is that they succumb far too often to the temptation to 'get someone to come in'. No school should ever do this without carrying out a rigorous due diligence audit of the individual or organisation concerned first. Most would fail. Teaching about social media and online safety almost always ends up being delivered by such people, entirely divorced from its real foundations, reading and writing in English.

At this point, it should be helpful to use an example of the kind of teaching that's missing. What are the kinds of issues and questions you need to address once you've made a decision to write and publish your own words on a platform? Each platform will be different, but it's the strategy I hope is useful. I'm going to use Twitter, but the same exercise would be applicable to any platform you care to name. This is the kind of discussion and information children need to understand before they commit themselves to writing English in sentences online, which, in

---

75. What happened to Amélie Wen Zhao's debut novel, *Blood Heir*, in January 2019 is a good example.

most cases, will be there for anyone to read even decades later. The consequences of this are of course considerable. For children to understand any of this, their teachers must too.

First, you need understand what your goals are. People will have different aims and purposes when they sign up to something, but knowing exactly what they are and sticking to them is vital. I wonder how many edu-tweeters have ever thought that through? I suspect a lot of the aggression, brick-wall debate and personal vilification would vanish if more users did actually know what their goals were. It helps, of course, to write them down and refer to them. Every platform is deliberately and cleverly designed to demand your attention and steal your time, so it had better be worth it. Using teachers as the obvious exemplar, what kinds of purposes might they have for using Twitter? Some might seek professional advice and information. Twitter is undoubtedly a place where the sharing of teaching resources and material is enabled. You can learn a lot from others doing the same work as you. Some might use Twitter as a career strategy. Having a Twitter identity is a way of being seen and known by others in a position to employ you, or of benefiting your career ambitions in other ways such as attending events and networking. In the entirely appropriate commercial jargon, it's about building a brand. The moment you make that decision, a whole lot of other questions naturally follow. Brands operate in specific ways. They are visible and consistent. They identify and target their consumers. They draft all their messages carefully and precisely to stay in keeping with the brand. All brands put themselves in a specific market and make sure potential buyers know where to find them. Broken down in this way, I'd hope any professional teacher might at this point be asking themselves, given Twitter's predilection for controversy and provocation, is it a wise choice to use it in preference to other platforms, if this is your aim?

Contrary to the career-minded user, some might simply want to remain anonymous and express their views and opinions freely. Reasons for doing so could be almost endless since Twitter as a platform doesn't specialise and embraces everything from the illiterate rantings of elected politicians to 'the best that has been thought and said', generously reproduced for you to consume by selfless advocates of civil discourse and culture. You might simply see it as entertainment. But that question – how much time is it worth investing? – should still be right at the forefront of your thinking because the moment you decide to sign up, you trigger a sequence of attention-seeking invitations that grow exponentially. If you leave your notifications on, for example, you will quickly be encouraged to pay attention minute by minute, regardless of whether you are in a meeting or the middle of a lesson. The device only cares about where you are if it means it can sell you something, harvest data about you or regain your attention.

Whatever your goals, they should determine what you write and how you express yourself in English. Anonymity offers licence that brands are never at liberty to enjoy. So powerful have platforms like Twitter become that thoughtful people are reporting a phenomenon new to the West: self-censorship. It might seem to some a small price to pay for bandwidth. Twitter offers you a vast readership; you just have to play by their arcane rules. Which is precisely why this kind of exercise is the proper responsibility of English teachers. Self-censorship is the death of literature. The moment you restrain your thought for fear of others' reactions, you are no longer free to think. If teaching English means teaching children how to write, it has to liberate them from this danger for life. Given that so much of what today's teenagers will write as adults will be published online, this is a serious matter. Far more serious than whether or not they can mimic other authors sufficiently well to be deemed 'creative'.

That Twitter test case could be applied to any online platform or app which offers you space to write. It hopefully illustrates not just the superficial communicative risks, but the profound implications for the way all schools teach English today. If we don't deal with these questions adequately and thoughtfully, what we actually risk is *unteaching* the ability to write. I see evidence of that already happening every week.

The risk to reading that technology presents is no less serious. As long ago as 2005, some researchers started to notice that reading from screens instead of hard copy was having an effect on the way children read. Ziming Liu from San Jose State University concluded, 'Screen-based reading behavior is characterized by more time spent on browsing and scanning, keyword spotting, one-time reading, non-linear reading, and reading more selectively, while less time is spent on in-depth reading, and concentrated reading. Decreasing sustained attention is also noted.'[76]

---

76. www.bit.ly/346fGby, accessed 17th February 2020.

Since then, Anne Mangen – a professor at the National Centre for Reading Education and Research at the University of Stavanger whose work focuses on the haptics of reading, both screen and in print – has stressed the breadth of choice that screen reading demands. That choice undermines the ability to read with the kind of undivided attention all English teachers know is necessary merely to enjoy a novel. Working memories struggle when distracted by hyperlinks, images and animation. With her colleagues, Mangen carried out a reading test that required students to read a short story in print and a Kindle e-book version which mimicked the type used in the hard copy and is free of links etc., the point being to make the screen and print experiences as visually similar as possible. When Mangen tested the readers' comprehension, she found the medium mattered a lot. Readers were asked to place a series of events from the story in chronological order, and the students who had read in print made far fewer mistakes and could recreate the story much more accurately.[77] Reading expert Maryanne Wolf, author of *Proust and the Squid*, has been especially vocal about the way screen reading may be hindering children's ability to read with the kind of skill that studying literature (or indeed any sophisticated prose) demands. Cognitive scientist Daniel Willingham in *The Reading Mind* expressed similar concerns, although he places more emphasis on the way technology has reduced children's patience or tolerance for demanding tasks like reading literary fiction. Julie Coiro, a professor in reading education at the University of Rhode Island, has also devoted her research effort into trying to understand the differences between reading from a screen and in print. Her work has focused on younger teenagers, and she too is confident that screen reading is a qualitatively different experience, offering children a bewildering choice that sitting with a book always excludes. Like Willingham, she argues that children need to learn how to read in both formats and that being a skilful reader in print does not mean you will be equally strong using a screen.

As someone with years of literary scholarship, teaching, research and business reading experience, I find the implications of all this research entirely straightforward. There are pragmatic, sequential issues here the

---

77. Mangen, Anne & Walgermo, Bente & Brønnick, Kolbjørn. (2013). 'Reading linear texts on paper versus computer screen: Effects on reading comprehension'. *International Journal of Educational Research*. 58. 61-68.

moment you ask that crucial question: what happens in the real world? If learning to read – not to decode but to *read* – is largely achieved by individual children engaging with a prose text for sustained periods – shutting out all distractions and focusing wholly on what is usually a fictional world, woven for them by a skilled author – then it follows that reading on screens has to happen later. Teaching a child to read from a screen is like shooting that child in their reading foot. If reading is primarily experienced not as imaginative surrender to someone else's prose, but as a series of decisions and choices determined by colour and movement – a matter of self-control more than imaginative pleasure – then surrendering to someone else's thoughts in prose becomes a mountain to climb. Children have to learn to read from books if they are to learn to read well at all. The only difference between reading a complex commercial or research document and reading a sophisticated novel is imaginative commitment…and enjoyment. Both require high levels of concentration and engagement with complex syntax, often difficult conceptual language and meandering narratives. At the most basic level, these texts are also lengthy and screens actively mitigate lengthy reading. Scrolling, like page turning, is a design limitation determined by size. But unlike turning a page, where the reader has a tangible sense of progress and movement through a text or narrative, scrolling carries with it the unattractive promise of infinity. Page numbers don't help because everyone who uses a screen has already learned 'the page' is effectively endless. There is always somewhere else to go. These profoundly important differences have to be understood and taught by real-world English teachers.

Reviewing Maryanne Wolf's new book, *Reader, Come Home: The Reading Brain in a Digital World*, Doug Lemov puts a premium on the risk every secondary school English teacher is facing when they teach children how to read:

> Reading taught us to sustain and logically develop ideas, to enter the minds and perspectives of others through their words. As societies, we became less impulsive, violent, and irrational. Wolf quotes Nicolo Machiavelli reflecting on how he lost himself in a book, conducting an inner dialogue with the author and reading for four hours without interruption.[78]

---

78. www.bit.ly/34kRgeD, accessed 18th February 2020.

If teenagers leave secondary education unable to approach anything like this level of reading, as so many do, can we confidently talk about having educated them? Have we already passed the tipping point where what schools produce instead are children with a completely different, more limited expectation? Lemov continues: 'Skittish, distracted readers rewire differently from thoughtful and meditative ones, and so they—and the collective "we"—come to think differently, to develop different architecture for thinking. Through disuse, we are losing what Wolf calls "cognitive patience", and thus the ability to immerse ourselves fully in books.'[79] Is this a price we can afford to pay as a society and culture? The risk is monumental and it's real. If English teachers don't fight this real-world battle, no one will, and what we collectively stand to lose is unthinkable. A slow, steady but inevitable trickling-away of significant knowledge from one generation to the next. History doesn't naturally immunise us from ignorance.

Quite quickly after I left the classroom and was embroiled in educational technology work, I found myself working in partnership with the Tate Gallery and the huge film archive British Pathé. I subsequently worked with a number of other galleries and museums as they slowly realised that technology was inevitably changing their relationship with the visiting and, more importantly, non-visiting public. On one occasion, listening to the educational lead at the British Museum talk about their various online projects, it struck me that we have teacher training all wrong – that the Victorians, the people who actually built most of those museums, galleries and archives, knew something we've forgotten. They fully appreciated the immense educational value of a physical artefact. They knew that contemplating a dried flower, an illuminated manuscript or just a lump of rock was fundamentally an educational act because, at the very least, it added to one's knowledge. Their appetite for collecting, cataloguing and listing was phenomenal and, as any modern curator will tell you, what is on display today is a tiny fraction of what we possess. There is an immense wealth of educational material stored up in the sector that as a nation we don't exploit anyway near as much as we should.

In a speech for the Institute for Public Policy Research in 2014, Dominic Cummings – the adviser who masterminded the successful

---

79. Ibid.

Brexit campaign (and, as some in the media would have it, the current UK government's evil puppet master) – talked about post-war Britain still lacking a role. His preference was for the UK to aim to become the global leader in education and science. He pointed out that we already have many of the best universities and schools. The rest of the world clearly agrees because international students flock to both.

If you consider something I've already discussed – the way good lessons are so often built around a single or series of educational assets[80] – then there is a completely logical connection between teaching and our great museum collections, archives and galleries. These organisations are, in essence, repositories of knowledge. Conventional textbooks in a whole range of subjects are already a halfway house between these two things. Good textbooks are full of reproductions of artefacts, more often than not objects held in these collections. Even science textbooks find invaluable material in these institutions. Why, then, do we not educate teachers in them? Many have already taken considerable steps to digitise their collections and make them far more accessible. Consider the message given out professionally: imagine if instead of being taught generic pedagogy and educational theory at a university, or being seduced by Teach First into thinking your job is 'to make a difference', subject specialist teachers were linked from the outset with prestigious institutions and organisations that own the educational assets which will form the centre of so many of their lessons to come. The museum and galleries sector complain constantly about shortage of funds. Is it really inconceivable to transfer money and responsibility for teacher training to them, from a university sector that is already bloated and criticised heavily for developing a wide range of courses the real world doesn't value? I asked the question myself at that British Museum conference years ago and was met with complete bemusement. I wonder if posing the same question today would get the same incredulous reaction. For far too long, the education sector has been seduced and fooled by technocratic thinking when it should have been challenging and demanding something *better* than repurposed business tools and data. Connecting teacher training to knowledge repositories is precisely that kind of better.

---

80. See above, p.74.

Regaining control

In this next section, I'll explore how schools and English teachers who decide to turn the tables on technology can regain control. In chapter one, I said, 'Technology tends to constrain language use, not liberate it.'[81] The pristine, blank sheets of paper you purchase in a diary offer a different kind of invitation to write than a text box. A diary made of paper says, 'Write in me,' while a mobile phone or computer screen always says, 'Write on me.' The diary is entirely and potently empty until you start to write. The other two are crammed full of invisible invitations to shift your attention away from writing to exchanging communication and enhancing the unadulterated text with additional material. What you write is never good enough for the mobile phone or the computer screen. They demand you add movement, colour, visual images or sound. If Silicon Valley could think of a way to replicate taste and smell, they would do that too. Every new device distracts users by offering choice. I've worked with dozens of IT technicians and engineers and, delightful though they are, many exhibit a particular trait which is intensely frustrating and which explains why this happens. On numerous occasions, I've been involved in projects that require me to explain to an engineer what a piece of new software needs to do to deliver an educational outcome. Almost always, after I've explained clearly and precisely what I want the application to do, the engineer would say, 'That's easy...but how about if it did this too?' It's almost impossible to rein in their enthusiasm for technology. There is always something more that can be added on, something extra an application can be made to do. I watched one quite successful edtech business fail essentially because no one could leave it alone. Something new was added month after month until the users, who were all busy school teachers, simply gave up because every time they went to use the application, there was something visibly unfamiliar and new they had to learn how to do.

All new technology requires behavioural change, and schools have been largely missing in action for two decades now in the battle to decide whether such change brings credible educational gains or not. It's a cliché in business world change management that 'culture eats strategy

---

81. See above, p.23.

for breakfast'. Yet schools repeatedly try to implement strategic changes without any understanding of the time they might require, the communications effort necessary or the likely educational impact. To take just one example, how many schools implemented interactive whiteboards in all classrooms without any realistic understanding of the scale of the change management challenge it involved? The same has been true of iPads for many schools. On one occasion, I was working in a school when a teacher approached me in the staffroom and asked me if I could have a look at her interactive whiteboard because although she'd had it almost 18 months, she'd never managed to get it working. She knew I worked for the company who manufactured it. I'm no technician, but for obvious reasons I took a look…and once I'd put some batteries in the pen, it worked fine. Factor in anything to do with technology and difficulties multiply. If you're going to implement change in a school that isn't likely to be easy for the majority of teachers to deliver, it will fail. The odds are stacked against you because teachers, like all other workers, range widely in ability, so anything a school decides to do must be within the grasp of a comfortable majority. This is an area where educational research has been minimal help because researchers so often design their projects in abstract, without fully understanding what happens on the ground, in real schools with real teachers and children. Whenever I read a research paper in which a researcher says they had to 'account for' something, I always ask myself one question: what was it in the real world they didn't like?

All English teachers who have ever decanted an entire class into an IT suite and set pupils a writing task will know exactly how little of value is achieved precisely because precious teaching time is squandered making unnecessary choices. I can remember the first time I did this myself. A class full of clever, fluent writers produced a handful of sentences in a bewildering array of fancy fonts and colours, when in their conventional exercise books they would have written two or more pages of articulate prose in black or blue ink. It follows that children shouldn't be introduced to technology for writing until they have a confident grasp of personal expression without it. If you put aside speech, the essential skill every school expects parents to put in place, handwriting must therefore come first. (Disturbingly, the UK Department for Education's follow-up survey to its *Childcare and Early Years Survey of Parents 2018*, published in February 2020, found that 14% of parents felt it was the responsibility of schools and childcare providers, not parents, to help children aged five and under to learn to speak, and this rose to 23% of parents in families earning under £20,000 per year.)[82]

For secondary schools, thinking seriously about handwriting means rejecting outright those innovative siren calls from the industry and its advocates to abandon handwritten exams in favour of technology. In any education system built around a series of high-stakes exams, the moment any of those exams requires using technology to write or submit answers to questions, teaching will inevitably change to reflect that. In search of exam success, teachers will unwittingly busy themselves *unteaching* writing. The retrospective impact will be deeply damaging. In the first two or three years of secondary school, many children are slow, deliberate writers still developing their own handwriting style. Knowing they face a series of high-stakes exams aged 16, all to be completed using a keyboard, would guarantee most of them never learn to write by hand at all. At the risk of upsetting half my readership, any Brit who has worked with US colleagues in business will be familiar with what happens to adults' handwriting when children use keyboards too early. But because writing prose is always more than the mechanics of penmanship – it's a complex activity involving vocabulary choice, punctuation, grammar knowledge and, pre-eminently, thought – if you teach children to write using a keyboard first, you risk killing their ability to think and write without the Swiss army knife-type crutch that technology provides. Social media is awash with English produced by Swiss army knife typists.

When I made the move from teaching to business, one of the habits I repeatedly noticed was how this manifested itself in the real world. It's almost unheard of for anyone in business to start from a blank page. There is always a spreadsheet, a template, a tool or a pre-existing document to turn to. A globally famous consultancy business I worked for had built its entire business model around this principle. If you worked for them and needed advice on how to interpret a set of accounts from a major airline or a minor airhead, someone, somewhere in the business would have a tool for it. Even researchers do this. Ignore all the naive nonsense from the OECD, politicians and Futurists who talk about the 21st-century skills children need to thrive in tomorrow's world of work (which they

---

82. www.bit.ly/2JKOW76, p.26, accessed 24th February 2020.

singularly lack themselves, having no experience of that world to base it on) – all that problem solving, collaboration, teamwork and creativity. In the real world, people have a near morbid terror of starting from scratch. I was often praised for being 'creative' by colleagues merely because I was an ex-English teacher naturally unintimidated by a white sheet of paper.

In real-world terms, as has already been touched on, this implies that secondary school English teachers have to embrace more responsibility for teaching handwriting formally than they might be used to. This doesn't necessarily mean expending lesson time reteaching cursive handwriting to children who leave primary school without it, but it does mean making sure every pupil attains a level of fluency, legibility and speed that allows them to participate fully in any exam they may take. It means telling them and teaching them that thinking and writing *by hand* is a fundamental skill on which much of their future academic or career success is built. It means explaining to them why it matters that they learn to write by hand *before* they inevitably move wholesale to a keyboard: because it is always primarily and literally a thoughtful process. Relying on a keyboard too soon risks stifling that vital ability to *think* before committing words to a page or screen. Discussions between professional writers about how they work are full of accounts about how much time it takes to produce the words, how many words they can write each day, what time of the day they write best and why. They are often obsessed with routines and rituals, with whether bourbons or garibaldis are more inspirational, because writing is always a thought-*full* business. Considerable time goes into each word. If you really want to teach a child how to write well, teach them how to think for themselves. Otherwise, you risk crippling their intellect.

Without doubt, the single action any school can take to help English teachers regain control is to remove mobile phones from teaching spaces completely. The French government considered this action so education-ally necessary that they made it law. French children cannot use their phones inside school premises or while they are on school-based activities outside of school like sporting events or trips. They are banned from connecting any device to the internet, with some exceptions for special needs children. The law applies to children from école maternelle (pre-school) up to the ninth graders in *collège* who are aged 15. At *lycée*, the last three years of high school, individual schools can operate their own rules about phones.

Technocratic arguments about this being backward or restrictive (because schools are stopping children using all those other amazingly 'cool' tools, the software applications and sources of information online that would help their studies) should end the moment anyone claiming to be a grown-up uses the word 'cool', which they inevitably do. They ignore the reality that none of these things matters more than the curriculum. Most spring from a decrepit constructivist ideology that IT breathed new life into and which believes children learn best by doing. In real-world terms, this commonly equates to experimentation and failure. All teachers begin every year in front of each class knowing there is a distinct body of information and knowledge they must convey in a limited time, which makes constructivism inherently anti-curriculum. Attempts have been made to design a constructivist curriculum in secondary school – most notably in the UK, the RSA's Opening Minds curriculum, but you need only look at its five core 'competences' to see where the risks lie. This is in itself a fascinating example of real-world English usage. The words 'competence' and 'competency' are often used interchangeably, even though attempts have been made to distinguish them. Most people might think of them as quite recent neologisms[83] and I was certainly unfamiliar with them until I started working in business, where they are commonly used by human resources professionals. But then the English teacher in me still cringes when he sees 'human resources' being used as a phrase to describe people whose job is to hire and fire. A bad euphemism is, after all, one which fails to hide something or fails to make you smile in the attempt. Taking these words out of the business world and transplanting them into schools is just another symptom of technocracy. It might well be useful to look at a potential employee's career for evidence of their ability to perform a specific role within an organisation or business, but is it really applicable to teenagers learning the basics of specific academic subjects? The employee is being assessed on their ability to perform a very narrow range of tasks, usually within an organisation that is itself tightly focused on a limited number of goals. The teenager is being assessed on a far wider range of skills and knowledge than they will ever be tested on again, and many would argue the whole business of schooling is to empower the individual and open up their opportunities. It's ironic that

---

83. 'Competence' actually dates from the 1590s and appears in Shakespeare, as does 'competency'.

the RSA chose to call its constructivist curriculum 'Opening Minds'. Its five competences are these:

- Citizenship
- Learning
- Managing information
- Relating to people
- Managing situations

Collectively, they reveal a distinct preference for employment as opposed to higher education or further study. Opening Minds also talks about 'open-ended' projects, which simply means that teaching subject knowledge becomes just another opportunity cost. Of course, there's a place in any secondary school for project work and experimentation. The problems come when technocrats, not subject specialist teachers, construct the entire curriculum. When the tables haven't been turned.

Regaining control means the relationship between technology and schools needs to be inverted. Technology businesses are not educational experts no matter how much research they fund, how much data they generate or how transformational the promises they successfully sell to politicians and the media. Schools and teachers can no longer sit back and let technology be imposed on them directly by commerce, or indirectly by government, without demanding credible evidence of educational value. Teachers need to insist they are the educational experts and challenge the web of relationships between business, lobbyists and politicians that has so successfully imposed its own will on them since that very first 'Why bother when you can just google it?' because – make no mistake – it isn't going to stop.

The EU recently issued a white paper, *On Artificial Intelligence – A European approach to excellence and trust*,[84] which indicates the direction of traffic. In the last three years, the commission spent €1.5 billion on research and innovation for AI. That was a 70% increase on its spending in the previous three years. The paper covers every possible use of AI and, in terms of education, talks mostly about making sure there will be enough programmers with the right knowledge and skills coming

---

84. www.bit.ly/2yO6For, accessed 20th February 2020.

through the university sector without having anything to say about schools. But it does talk about providing better public services and specifically reducing the cost of providing those public services, mentioning education alongside transport, energy and waste management. The ambition is to make sure EU countries are able to compete and contribute to what the paper believes is an inevitable explosion of AI technology globally. One of its key proposals is the creation of a *lighthouse* research centre for Europe (those crucial single words again) to attract talent and spread excellence globally, but the most pertinent section for teachers is this reference under a section on skills:

> The updated Digital Education Action Plan will help make better use of data and AI-based technologies such as learning and predictive analytics with the aim to improve education and training systems and make them fit for the digital age. The Plan will also increase awareness of AI at all levels of education in order to prepare citizens for informed decisions that will be increasingly affected by AI.[85]

Teachers are citizens too. The paper refers to ethics and citizens quite a lot, but dataism is its core faith, and there is no doubt that the EU is happy to align its interests with those technology businesses who have so successfully sold 'AI' as something dramatic and revolutionary, so it's worth sharing what the EU thinks it is. Of the three different definitions referred to in the paper, the simplest describes AI as 'a collection of technologies that combine data, algorithms and computing power'. So much for the hype. There is a second, more bureaucratic definition that is equally useful as a balance to the rhetoric more common in advertising and from the gurus and technocrats in education set on making teachers and schools feel inferior and outmoded, yet again:

> Artificial intelligence (AI) refers to systems that display intelligent behaviour by analysing their environment and taking actions – with some degree of autonomy – to achieve specific goals. AI-based systems can be purely software-based, acting

---

85. Ibid, p.6.

in the virtual world (e.g. voice assistants, image analysis software, search engines, speech and face recognition systems) or AI can be embedded in hardware devices (e.g. advanced robots, autonomous cars, drones or Internet of Things applications).[86]

The vital information here are those two points about 'autonomy' and 'intelligent behaviour', although any room full of teachers would be entertained for hours if anyone asked them to define 'intelligent behaviour'. A third, high-level expert group definition goes further and does an even better job of demystifying what's really happening when a Silicon Valley executive steps up to the mike and starts telling everyone how excited they are:

Artificial intelligence (AI) systems are software (and possibly also hardware) systems designed by humans that, given a complex goal, act in the physical or digital dimension by perceiving their environment through data acquisition, interpreting the collected structured or unstructured data, reasoning on the knowledge, or processing the information, derived from this data and deciding the best action(s) to take to achieve the given goal. AI systems can either use symbolic rules or learn a numeric model, and they can also adapt their behaviour by analysing how the environment is affected by their previous actions.[87]

I'll attempt to make that even clearer because if schools and teachers are to regain control then they really do need to know what someone's trying to sell. An AI machine or application has the ability to do what someone tells it to do by gathering data and making decisions based on that data. It can also decide again based on new data. It cannot *reason*, beyond making calculations you've enabled it to make, nor can it choose the *best* action beyond the range of actions determined by the goal you set it.

An informative example at the most sophisticated end of AI is the widely reported AlphaGo program built by the company DeepMind. This program learned to play the board game Go in a matter of days

---

86. Ibid, p. 16.
87. Ibid, p. 16.

then defeated one of the world's top players. The program succeeded in identifying new knowledge then developed unconventional strategies and completely new moves. Understanding how it did that should help demystify the whole AI world. AlphaGo was given a goal (winning Go) and the ability to play the game: it was taught the rules and what constituted a legal move. It played the game against itself and remembered what it had done, each time using an algorithm to improve its performance, so the quality of its self-play increased. After every game, the interaction between the algorithm instructing it to win and the updated version of what it had remembered created a new, better version of itself again and again. It could update its ability to predict successful moves and the eventual winner of the game at such a speed that it effectively learned how to beat the world's best player in three days. Now that wasn't so painful, was it.

Teachers should know what AI really is so that when it comes knocking on their door as the next best thing, or when someone at a low-budget-Davos event in Dubai starts talking about replacing teachers with AI, they can challenge its use and decide for themselves whether or not it might deliver any educationally valuable outcomes. Civil society needs its professional teachers to stand up, ask the hard questions and demand credible answers because, of course, no one else will be able to until they do. The most likely form it will take is 'adaptive' technology. This is sold as technology which (through testing and analysing the data produced against huge data sets) can predict an individual child's educational need. It adapts the resource or test it gives them because it's able to position them accurately on a predetermined scale of performance. In my experience as a teacher and someone who has worked with a lot of new technology, adaptive learning is an extraordinarily crude, 'one step up, one step down' process. It always thinks of learning as a ladder, not a journey. Try climbing a ladder more than two rungs at a time.

Linguistic lawlessness

One of the most pernicious and worrying real-world changes new technology has brought goes right to the heart of what it means to be an English teacher, to the core of the social and cultural responsibility all English teachers bear. It's arguably the most significant gap in real-world English teaching, which is why I have saved it for last. When Lewis Carroll put the following words into Humpty Dumpty's mouth in *Through the Looking-Glass*, he was writing for children. A scholarly mathematician, Carroll knew the value of precision and rules.

> 'When I use a word,' Humpty Dumpty said, in rather a scornful tone, 'it means just what I choose it to mean – neither more nor less.'
> 'The question is,' said Alice, 'whether you can make words mean so many different things.'
> 'The question is,' said Humpty Dumpty, 'which is to be master – that's all.'

One hundred and fifty years later and, with the help of technology, the real world is now overrun by Humpty Dumptys. Wherever you care to look, you will find evidence of a linguistic lawlessness that would have bemused Carroll and his contemporaries. It's there in the media – social and mainstream – politics, academia and the arts. Even big business isn't immune. It's no accident that this passage has been repeatedly cited in court cases and legal argument ever since Alice first challenged Humpty Dumpty's egocentric laxity. Working closely with commercial lawyers teaches you that the law is often little more than a dispute between clever individuals about what words mean. Carroll was fascinated by logic and puzzles, and in one of his scholarly works on logic he wrote that as long as an author explains beforehand that when he uses the word 'black' he will always mean 'white', and that when he uses the word 'white' he means 'black', he would be perfectly happy to go along. Through Humpty, Carroll takes the etymological reality that words change to its logical conclusion. Once upon a time, it was perfectly possible to be kempt, flappable and even ept, because words, like the times, change. But that's all Carroll's exchange between Alice and Humpty Dumpty is: an amusing exercise in logic. Alice is the voice of reason intimating the resulting communicative chaos in a world full of Humptys, the real world we all now contend with.

Journalism has moved from a place where it was a reasonably respected profession – rooted in investigative objectivity and impartiality, a section of civil society that in the US merits the honour of being called 'the fourth estate' – to being indistinguishable from politics itself and, at its worst, nothing more illuminating than ill-educated activism. The massive shift of news reporting online has seen the title 'journalist' co-opted by all kinds of individuals who publish prose via the internet but who lack professional experience and the important values that conventionally accompany the job. Nonetheless, they are invited to participate in discussions by major news channels who have themselves seen their standards of journalism weakened and undermined by the same online shift. Channel 4's head of news, Dorothy Byrne (a professional journalist), speaking at the Edinburgh Festival in 2019, called Boris Johnson 'a proven liar' – a phrase which must have given her legal colleagues palpitations. Subsequently, when Johnson chose not to appear in a climate change debate between leadership candidates *Channel 4 News* organised during the 2019 election, Byrne no doubt felt they were behaving professionally when they substituted an ice sculpture in his stead. Eight weeks into government and Boris Johnson announced that Channel 4, which is funded by the state, would be sold.[88] The BBC, the world's gold standard in journalism, has itself come under intense government scrutiny for what many perceive as political bias. When Humptys decide what the word 'journalist' means and then go on to embed that habit in their writing, and when there are not enough Alices to challenge them, the consequences can be dramatic, even for institutions as famous and powerful as the BBC. Listen to or watch any major news channel any day of the week and I defy any English teacher not to find their ears tingling at some point as they think, 'Hold on! That's not what the word means.'

A number of organisations have carried out surveys to try to establish an accurate view of whether or not the BBC has maintained its impartiality as technology has ruffled the waves they once confidently ruled. Perhaps the most neutral is Ofcom, the UK government's regulatory body for the communications industry. Ofcom has a statutory duty to represent the interests of citizens and consumers by promoting competition and protecting the public from harmful or offensive material, so it's only reasonable to expect them to be rigorous in anything they say about political bias in broadcasting. In their 2019 *News Consumption* report, Ofcom found that 71% of viewers felt BBC TV news was 'trustworthy' and that 59% felt it was 'impartial'. Those figures sound impressive but more people thought the same of ITV (74%), Sky News (73%) and CNN

---

88. Byrne subsequently stood down from Channel 4 in March 2020.

(74%). While 59% thought BBC TV was 'impartial', other major channels did even better: ITV (65%), Sky News (68%), Channel 4 (65%) and CNN (70%). Only Channel 5 did worse than the BBC on 58%.[89] In 2018, the market researchers BMG carried out a more specific poll that asked a representative sample of just over one thousand British adults to what extent, if at all, they believed that the UK's largest television broadcasters (the BBC, Sky, ITV, Channel 4, and RT) were biased or politically neutral. They concluded that the data revealed considerable partisan effects so that people's perception of bias for any one news channel, including the BBC, mirrored their own politics. The data did, however, position ITV and Channel 4 as more politically neutral than the BBC, and the survey's authors found that marginally more viewers believed the BBC exhibited a left-wing bias than believed there was a right-wing one. The Centre for Policy Studies, a centre-right think tank, published the report *Bias at the Beeb? A Quantitative Study of Slant in BBC Online Reporting* in August 2013 and concluded simply that 'the BBC exhibits a left-of-centre slant in its online reporting'.[90] You will no doubt have your own experience of BBC reporting to juxtapose against the various findings of these surveys.

Academia is equally troubled by linguistic lawlessness. This is one of those intriguing areas where American English and British English part company to some degree. It's not unusual to find US academics tacking the word 'violence' on to a list of otherwise perfectly innocent terms, so sociologists will refer to 'data violence', post-colonialist academics will discuss 'epistemic violence' and lawyers 'administrative violence'. For those of us who are fortunate enough to live our lives entirely or largely free from violence, such usage is jarringly hyperbolic. Violence is associated by Alices with physical harm and damage, often extreme, not least because we are most familiar with it from the internet, cinema and television, in spite of the Obscene Publications Act which exists to protect citizens from dramatised and, on rare occasions, real depictions of violence. When academics use the term like this, they are deliberately provoking the Alice in us to make a connection they want us to make for their own rhetorical ends. They want to us to feel the same abhorrence for 'data violence' or 'epistemic violence' that they do, so they connect it with

89. www.bit.ly/34k3XXi, p. 74, accessed 24th February, 2020.
90. www.bit.ly/2JMRgdT, p. 14, accessed 24th February, 2020.

what they know we already naturally abhor. Like Humpty, they believe they are masters of the word.

Another word used widely in the US academic circles, but less so in English ones, is 'gaslighting'. The word is a particularly useful example of linguistic lawlessness because it has a distinctly traceable recent history. It derives its meaning, if you exclude it referring to how streets were illuminated before electricity, from a 1938 stage play by the English author Patrick Hamilton called *Gas Light*. In the play, a husband who has already murdered one woman for her jewels, undermines his wife's sanity by consciously and deliberately lying to her to convince her and others that she is mentally unstable. The gas lights in their apartment go dim when he secretly goes upstairs to search for the jewels of the woman he's murdered and uses the gas light in her rooms, but he skilfully tells his wife she is imagining the lights dimming in theirs. With this play later made into a popular and successful film by the famous Hollywood director George Cukor, the idea of deliberately lying to someone to confuse and manipulate them embedded itself in popular culture and film theory as 'gaslighting'. In some academic work, you will find it being used much more loosely to describe any act of undue influence or pressure, often exerted by a majority group over a minority who, it's usually argued, are being oppressed. The word 'erase' has also been coerced in this Humpty Dumpty manner when academics want to argue that certain cultural practices or representations exclude minorities. Grown-up Alice would expect the word to be reserved for either mundane practical situations to do with drawing or print, or – much more dramatic – wholescale human events such as genocide or totalitarian censorship.

These are common examples, but the Humpty Dumpty strategy is contagious in the real world, and you will find it almost anywhere you care to look when English is being used to persuade or convince. A UK higher education think tank, commenting on the admissions scandal that rocked elite US universities in 2019, tweeted these precise words:

> Corruption A: bribing a university sports coach to admit your child. Illegal.

> Corruption B: parents paying up to $2.5 million to 'sponsor' a university coaching position while your child applies to the same institution. Entirely legal and actively encouraged by the top unis.

One of the many things my real-world experience has provided is professional training in EU and UK fraud and anti-corruption legislation, so when a higher education think tank uses the word 'corruption' to describe something which they also know is 'entirely legal', my linguistic lawlessness hackles rise. This is linguistic lawlessness at its most blatant. One of the UK's major banks has done something very similar by using the expression 'We are not an island' to describe the UK in a major advertising campaign. The last time I needed to get to the continent, walking wasn't an option. It would be easy for English teachers to regard this echo of John Donne as sophisticated when something far less cultured is really going on. Donne's profoundly troubled Christianity is given a trite political makeover merely to align a major bank with its perceived customers. There is something deeply disturbing about the assertiveness of this kind of polarised transposition. It's as though the authors have no respect for language at all.

A small, select group of denotative words have been subjected to this strategy so commonly and ubiquitously, they've become impossible accusations to refute, yet simultaneously devoid of useful meaning. 'Racist', 'sexist', 'fascist' (and its synonym 'Nazi') are used (with a truly terrible irony) in the same way yellow stars were used to dehumanise Jews by real fascists. They are hurled at total strangers online, and even by the mainstream media, as a badge of dishonour, a visible mark of shame. They really are scarlet letters because those who hurl them so liberally know the accusation will stick if enough people agree by sharing or 'liking'. These words became effectively defunct the moment they began being used not as a descriptive nouns but as accusations of secular sacrilege. Democracy relies on free speech and respectful debate – principles denied and repressed by such linguistic lawlessness. In the real world, if English teachers don't nip this lexical degradation in the bud, no one will. The onus is on all those who teach adolescents how to use English in their speech and writing to instil a profound sense of linguistic integrity in them, to teach them what happens to debate and free speech in the real world when words become Humptys' playthings. This is why it's so important to teach linguistic history and etymology in those first few years in secondary school, to develop their knowledge *about* the language you hope they will use to good effect in later life. The solipsism inherent in so much English teaching that focuses on creativity needs to be replaced by a shared sense of linguistic responsibility, a mutual recognition of the widespread social and cultural damage ill-disciplined language causes. Teenagers entering the real world need real-world knowledge.

Once you become aware of lexical degradation, it's not difficult to find examples. While working on the Building Schools for the Future programme over a decade ago, I found myself wincing when builders and architects started referring to schools as 'communities' constantly – not because schools aren't communities, but because what they meant by it was something completely different and far weaker than I would have meant, using the same word. They used it as clever, commercial shorthand, because they knew it would meet with the approval of those political appointees overseeing the programme, not because it conveyed something important about the nature of a good school. More recently, the author Julie Burchill has also noted the word's degradation: '"Community" used to be such a jolly word, redolent of cheery singing or a nice place to land on the Monopoly board. Now it just means a bunch of whiners whining about stuff.'[91] 'Toxic,' 'bullying', even the word 'family' are all significant words and concepts that have been degraded, with grave social and cultural consequences. I can best illustrate why it matters with the word 'bullying'. There is no agreed legal definition of bullying, although the Department for Education offers a reasonably accurate one for schools to refer to. They define it as behaviour that is:

- repeated
- intended to hurt someone either physically or emotionally
- often aimed at certain groups, for example because of race, religion, gender or sexual orientation[92]

They are wrong only in their last bullet. In schools, it's very rarely associated with groups or minorities; that is an entirely political judgement, not an educational one. Bullying in schools is almost always an intensely personal issue, one individual who exhibits a profound antipathy for another, rooted in deeply personal characteristics. It's never a single event. It can have varied causes that amateur psychologists and bully apologists can fight over as much as they wish, but it usually stems from just two:

91. www.bit.ly/2y08t0G, accessed 26th February, 2020.
92. www.bit.ly/2XnhhbJ, accessed 26th February, 2020.

fear and envy. Bullies rarely act alone. They often coerce others to join in, either wittingly or unwittingly, because the whole point of the exercise is to destroy the victim's status and credibility within the peer group or community. If, as a teacher or a school community, you don't understand this, if 'bullying' is used to describe every minor playground tiff between children or arguments about dirty mugs in the staffroom, you will never deal with the real thing effectively.

Among the things I speak about at educational conferences are the problems with educational research design. Far too often, the design process shows no credible understanding of the real world of schools, teachers and pupils. I recently had a positive online discussion about this with the Associate Professor in Mathematics Education at the University of Southampton, Dr Christian Bokhove, because he is currently conducting research into school bullying in six countries. He acknowledged that lacking a definition and relying on self-reporting by pupils was a weakness, but his hope was that by asking multiple questions, they would be able to determine the extent of bullying. I'm less optimistic, in large part because of the lexical degradation the word has been subjected to. Left to their own devices, pupils will report everything from a stolen banana at lunchtime to late-night, anonymous, online abuse as 'bullying'. In the end, the researchers will be having to draw conclusions on data which is about general poor behaviour, not 'bullying'. This really does matter, because in the real world, bullying is extraordinarily difficult to put an end to. Bullies are Olympian in their focus and tenacity. Like alcoholics, sincerely reciting the Serenity Prayer is often the best they can ever hope for. There are only two ways to defeat them: either the community as a whole empowers the victim, or you prevent victim and bully from ever meeting. This is why I found that insipid BSF use of 'community' to describe schools so objectionable, because in a healthy school community, bullying is cultural anathema. If it does raise its ugly head, it's quickly and communally decapitated by peer pressure, as much as by the adults.

Whereas the lexical degradation of 'bullying' has pernicious consequences, mainly in schools, the most egregious example of this phenomenon in the real world is what has happened to the word 'hate'. Etymologically, the word has an intriguing history. The Old English word *hete* has Germanic and Norse origins. It was associated with spite and envy and indicated extreme hostility. It has never, until now, been a word wielded lightly. The phrase 'hate mail' only appeared in 1951, 'hate crime' as recently as 1988 and 'hate speech' not until the 1990s. The introduction of legislation that attempts to criminalise some uses of language as hate crimes must be one of the most naive, ill-informed acts a UK parliament has ever introduced. As the law currently stands, there are five protected categories (at least for the moment, because of course the second you grant special status to any group, others will seek equity under the law – which is precisely what has happened). The five are:

- disability
- race
- religion
- transgender identity
- sexual orientation

The decision to protect people who identify their gender in their own terms has proved so problematic, it has undermined the entire world of female sport, thrown clothes shops into utter confusion and produced a world in which the words 'man' and 'woman' have themselves become literally useless. None of this legislation was necessary because the behaviour it sought to police was already limited by legislation under the following categories:

Public order
Racial and religious hatred
Protection from harassment
Communications
Malicious communications

As things stand, a hate crime in England is defined as:

> Any criminal offence which is **perceived** by the victim or any other person, to be motivated by hostility or prejudice based on a person's race or **perceived** race; religion or **perceived** religion; sexual orientation or **perceived** sexual orientation; disability or **perceived** disability and any crime motivated by hostility or prejudice against a person who is transgender or **perceived** to be transgender.[93]

---

93. www.bit.ly/2y0jejA, accessed 26th February, 2020.

The bold type is mine and is there to stress that far from being the dysto-pian fictional creation of George Orwell, thought crime is now a real-world risk we all run. Perception is *not* objective truth and motivation is thought, *not* action. Police attempts to enforce this legislation have led to some high-profile court cases and plenty of voices have been raised questioning why they would pursue anyone for what they think, or even tweet, when there are far more serious crimes to investigate. The reason is both linguistic and historical. The 1999 Macpherson Report following the brutal murder of the black teenager Stephen Lawrence concluded that the Metropolitan Police Service was 'institutionally racist' and even defined that as:

> The collective failure of an organization to provide an appropri-ate and professional service to people because of their colour, culture, or ethnic origin. It can be seen or detected in pro-cesses, attitudes and behaviour which amount to discrimination through unwitting prejudice, ignorance, thoughtlessness and racist stereotyping which disadvantage minority ethnic people.[94]

Far more significantly, the report made one specific recommendation that led directly to hate crime legislation. It defined a racist incident as 'any incident which is **perceived** to be racist by the victim or any other person'.[95] Again the bold type is mine. At the stroke of a keyboard, the bedrock idea that for a crime to be committed, some form of human action is necessary, was completely overturned. Perception, not action, is all that is now required to determine a hate crime has been committed. It's a straight but perniciously slippery slope from the Macpherson Report to the Metropolitan Police Service's current definition of hate crime. It's almost like someone was using a template.

The undiluted folly of actually believing it's possible to police what peo-ple think was exposed brilliantly by John Milton in *Areopagitica*. Arguing against the desire by Cromwell's Puritan government to introduce the wholesale censorship of written works by the state, Milton had this to say about why such an idea is universally both foolish and futile:

---

94. www.bit.ly/2y1COfj, para, 6.34, accessed 26th February, 2020.
95. Ibid, Chapter 47, para 12.

They are not skilfull considerers of human things, who imagin to remove sin by removing the matter of sin Though ye take from a covetous man all his treasure, he has yet one jewell left, ye cannot bereave him of his covetousnesse. Banish all objects of lust, shut up all youth into the severest discipline that can be exercis'd in any hermitage, ye cannot make them chaste, that came not thither so.[96]

The way sensitivity reading has backfired on the YA publishing industry proves him right. If you really want to stifle an author's creativity, just tell them they mustn't offend anyone. Self-censorship is increasingly killing the arts. A recent survey by the UK publication *ArtsProfessional* of over 500 of its professional members working in the wider arts sector revealed just how suffocating the climate is:

Our arts, culture, and indeed education sectors are supposed to be fearlessly free-thinking and open to a wide range of challenging views. However, they are now dominated by a monolithic politically correct class (mostly of privileged white middle class people, by the way), who impose their intolerant views across those sectors.

This is driving people who disagree away, risks increasing support for the very things this culturally dominant class professes to stand against, and is slowly destroying our society and culture from the inside.[97]

The survey also highlighted what kinds of topics suffered from self-censorship. None of them will come as a surprise:

The research indicates the arts and cultural sector is intolerant of viewpoints outside of the dominant norms. Anything that might be considered 'politically incorrect' to the liberal-leaning sector – including expressing support or sympathy for Brexit,

---

96. John Milton, *Areopagitica*, www.bit.ly/34p69ga, accessed 26th February, 2020.
97. www.bit.ly/2JQ8uHq, accessed 26th February, 2020.

the Conservatives or other right-wing political parties – was felt to be risky territory.

Religion, gender and sexuality were also considered a 'minefield' and no-go areas for many: 'Anything to do with gender issues, especially trans issues, will get a lot of flak for either not being on message enough, or being off message, or too on message,' one person said.[98]

It seems you don't have to burn books these days. Just make sure they don't get written. 80% of the respondents thought that anyone in the sector who shared controversial opinions risked being professionally ostracised. Thinking back to chapter one, is it really such an unfair question to ask how we reached such a dire situation when English teaching puts such an emphasis on creativity? What kind of cultural madness possesses a major publishing house like Penguin Random House[99] so that it believes a policy selecting new authors on the basis of their ethnicity, gender, sexuality, social mobility and disability would generate literature worth reading? As the author Lionel Shriver pointed out in an interview with *The Guardian*, 'The texture of this procedural innovation is Soviet. If books don't adhere to the party line, they'll not see print, and the authors will be re-educated. That's what's already happening in YA fiction.'[100]

Business is just as vulnerable to the side effects of this linguistic lawlessness. Corporate giant Proctor and Gamble discovered early in 2019 that even a slight tweak to a long-standing successful marketing tag by one of its most famous brands, Gillette – 'The best a man can get' – had calamitous commercial consequences. It had to write down the value of the brand after a new campaign built around the revised tag – 'The best a man can be' – was poorly received by its own customers. In chapter one, I pointed out using the single word 'gent's' to describe a watch on eBay instead of 'men's' increased its value by $40. That tiny little 'be' cost Proctor and Gamble $8 billion, the sum they wrote down the value of Gillette at in 2019. In the key ad that caused all the furore, unsurprisingly

98. Ibid.
99. In 2019, Penguin announced its new inclusion policy, full details can be found here: www.bit.ly/3aOOAs6, accessed 28th February, 2020.
100. www.bit.ly/2woei7X, accessed 26th February, 2020.

the words 'toxic' and 'bullying' both made an appearance. Even though it's essentially a conventional before and after ad, the skilfully made short film depicts an array of unpleasant, aggressive behaviour by men in the workplace, at home and in public, in an effort to convince its customers they can be better. Apparently, it didn't occur to anyone in the advertising agency or Gillette that most of their customers do not behave in the ugly, clichéd manner the film insisted they do and they resented being scolded.

All of the above examples demonstrate that words have immense real-world consequences, that English usage really does matter. Teachers use the word 'lesson' most usually to describe those periods of the working day timetabled for them to appear in front of a group of children and teach the subject. But they all also know the word has a much broader cultural meaning and value, that lessons can be significant, lifelong possessions. However many timetabled English lessons they may have attended, if school leavers don't enter the real world having learned this lifelong lesson about language, have they really been properly prepared? If they succeeded in writing a brief piece of fiction in a GCSE exam, strung together a coherent argument or demonstrated that they understood a newspaper article by answering a series of questions about it, but had no sense of being held responsible as adults for what they say and write, how well educated were they? They should believe the English language is a rich and powerful gift, not a toy. They need to learn that they are all stewards of the language, free to embrace, challenge or reject new coinages or uses. They must appreciate language change is not always beneficial and that people will deliberately try to impose change for unethical purposes, and that unless they remain alert, they risk being victims. They should be aware that technology has automated what was previously a natural process rooted in face-to-face conversation and, much later print, so that the process can happen in days rather than decades. Words are not playthings, the Lego blocks of language. They are the currency of intelligence. When we ignore or turn a blind eye to manipulative or deceitful language, we degrade everyone's ability to communicate effectively. We are fast trying to undo the terrible consequences of polluting the physical environment we inhabit; we need to act equally exigently about cleaning up the English language.

The consequences of not doing so are most evident on social and other media. When I first started writing a column about education for *Tes*, I was quite interested in looking at the comments from their

Facebook users. As an author, I necessarily use a limited range of social media platforms (most notably Goodreads, LinkedIn and Twitter), but I quickly noticed something that distinguished these various platforms. Exactly the same column would provoke quite different response types on each. Although large numbers internationally would read the piece on LinkedIn, very few would ever comment, and those who did were always complimentary. Twitter readership was often much larger, predominantly UK-based; again there would be few comments, but there was definitely more likelihood some would be negative, dismissive or, on the odd occasion, openly antagonistic. By far the most comments would always appear on Facebook, where I could guarantee most would be UK-based and negative – many openly aggressive and unpleasant. Most striking of all, it was crystal clear, when you read their comments, that FB readers, presumably all professional teachers, were responding *not* to the full article, but only to the headline, which of course I never wrote. This was so obvious that I gave up looking at Facebook responses. There was simply nothing to be gained. On some of these platforms, a lie can put a girdle round the earth twice before the truth has reached out from under the sheets to slap the alarm clock. This should be of immense concern to English teachers because so much of what they do deals with discerning truths. When they ask pupils to study news reports or magazine features, when they teach those first tentative steps in literary criticism, the fundamental question is the same: how true is this? Condoning organisations that display no sense of linguistic or editorial responsibility, or colluding uncritically with them, is professionally paradoxical. Civility – civil society, if you will – had no one to speak for it when Silicon Valley came knocking; and teachers, most pertinently teachers of English, stepped quietly aside when, as stewards of the language, they should have been screaming, 'Stop right there!'. It's not too late. As we've seen when it comes to AI, politicians will only ever challenge technology if they believe it will secure them public support. They have nothing like the professional and ethical incentive English teachers have to play this role. At a time when some politicians are beginning to discuss reining in the technological excesses that have sown so much confusion, doubt and insecurity, English teachers should start to make their own voice heard and assert their status as the people responsible for making sure the next generation is suitably prepared to defend itself.

This harks back to earlier discussions about democracy and free speech. Most people agree without hesitation that democracy without free speech is impossible. Far fewer appear willing to defend the right to speak freely of anyone whose opinions and views they personally dislike. There is no halfway house. John Stuart Mill expressed this perfectly in *On Liberty* when he wrote:

> The peculiar evil of silencing the expression of an opinion is, that it is robbing the human race; posterity as well as the existing generation; those who dissent from the opinion, still more than those who hold it. If the opinion is right, they are deprived of the opportunity of exchanging error for truth: if wrong, they lose, what is almost as great a benefit, the clearer perception and livelier impression of truth, produced by its collision with error.[101]

You either embrace the necessity that some people may express ideas you find personally objectionable, because in so doing you are part of a much greater, civilised endeavour to pursue truth; or you don't think truth matters. In which case, why teach English? There are no 'buts' when it comes to free speech – ever.

Teaching English wouldn't normally figure especially highly in any employment roll of honour. The public admires both the knowledge and skill of a surgeon, the dedication and talent of a sports star, and sometimes even just the sheer gall of a celebrity, but the thousands of men and women who choose to teach English are grist to the employment mill, just more grubby white collars. No one stops to really consider their profound impact on our society and culture, the depth or frequency of the ripples they start. Silicon Valley has ironically done them a favour. By usurping the credibility of language itself, technology has reminded us just how important it is that we nurture and maintain the English language well. If schools fail to instil in children a sense of linguistic probity, a desire to use words with care and integrity, they undermine their future success personally and professionally. They send them out into the real world not as free citizens but as serfs.

---

101. www.bit.ly/39TutIb, p.19, accessed 28th February, 2020.

APPENDIX

What this entire book points to is an urgent need to reassess the real-world rationale for studying English in secondary education and rethink what teaching English in the secondary school should consist of. Throughout the book, I've suggested a number of subject areas that need addressing, rebalancing or fundamentally rethinking, and it seems only sensible to draw them all together here in a useful format. Below, you will find every key suggestion made in the preceding pages reproduced as precisely as possible, together with indications about what it implies for anyone teaching secondary English. You won't find any colourful graphics or digital rhetoric. What you read will be as unconstrained by the technology used to produce it as possible. The words, I hope, will be allowed to speak freely and honestly for themselves.

1. THINK ABOUT HOW TECHNOLOGY TENDS TO CONSTRAIN LANGUAGE USE, NOT LIBERATE IT.

Every device or software application children are likely to encounter that offers them the opportunity to write will also offer them multiple additional opportunities to think about choice, instead of thinking about the words best suited to convey their thought.

2. FIND AUTHENTIC WRITING TASKS FOR PUPILS IF AT ALL POSSIBLE.

You can teach children to write mechanistically by copying and modelling every possible semantic unit or literary device, and many will be able to reproduce what they have learned. But the difference between teaching this kind of writing and teaching real writing is akin to the difference between teaching a child to decode and teaching them to read. If you want to teach them to be comfortable with the idea of expressing themselves through writing, then finding tasks which they perceive as authentic is vital. They need good reason to write because good writing doesn't happen without a lot of thought.

3. STRESS THAT KNOWLEDGE ABOUT GRAMMAR IS KNOWLEDGE WORTH HAVING, JUST LIKE ALL OTHER SUBJECT KNOWLEDGE.

The ability to discuss the mechanics of a text, and therefore to learn from unfamiliar examples, is made much easier when you have the correct vocabulary to do so. Assimilating knowledge about grammar means children can participate much more successfully in all linguistic and literary discussion because they are not having to guess or invent the terms to use. Linguistic integrity makes more sense when you have strong knowledge about grammar.

4. FIND WAYS TO ENCOURAGE THEM TO THINK RATHER THAN MERELY SCAFFOLDING THEIR WRITING FOR THEM.

Teachers should appreciate just how difficult it is to write when most of the contact you have outside school actively discourages intellectual engagement. Teenagers are novices at almost everything and especially at thinking for themselves. Seek out and select material, information and activities that invite them to ponder and reflect, to invest time, *before* they try to capture their thought in writing. Modelling has a place but also carries the substantial risk that you actively prevent them thinking.

5. THINK EMPATHETICALLY ABOUT TEENAGERS' LIVES SO YOU CAN DESIGN AUTHENTIC WRITING AND GIVE THEM REASONS TO THINK.

If you invest time to understand those ideas and interests that engage the children you teach at any one time, you are more likely to be able to design authentic writing tasks for them. There is a professional line to be drawn between using your own passion for the subject to stimulate their interest and imposing your own opinions on them through the texts you select.

6. CONSIDER DIARY WRITING AS A MODEL WAY TO THINK ABOUT AUTHENTIC WRITING.

Diary writing is an ideal task in terms of authenticity and empathy. It reduces thinking time because it provides a wealth of immediately available, personal information to write about and it exploits the reality that, for most children, school is about friendships. It also implies that what they write has value.

7. ACCEPT THAT MOST OF THEIR WRITING ALREADY HAPPENS ON THEIR PHONE.

By the time most children start secondary school, they will already be doing most of their writing on a phone, and this has serious implications for how teachers develop their ability to write by hand. Mobile phones are not designed to facilitate high-quality writing. They are designed to seek and maintain your attention. It's only sensible, therefore, that English teachers, who bear the main responsibility for teaching high-quality writing, play a leading role in determining the whole school's attitude towards them.

8. LESSONS ON SOCIAL MEDIA SHOULD BE TAUGHT BY THE ENGLISH DEPARTMENT, NOT EXTERNAL VISITORS OR PSHE.

Social media platforms present all users with both opportunities and risks. Understanding and articulating those to pupils is the English department's job because PSHE and external advisers will have their own agendas, which are likely to clash with, or directly counter, the work of every English department. If children aren't taught about social media within the context of studying English, they are simply not being taught what they will need to know in the real world.

9. TELL THEM THAT EDITING REALLY MATTERS BECAUSE THERE IS NO GOING BACK ONCE YOU PRESS SEND.

The speed with which real-world technology allows things to be written and published means it's crucial that children learn the importance of editing as an integral part of the writing process. They need to learn that there is an important distinction between proofreading and editing, that anything which hasn't been rigorously edited hasn't been properly written.

10. TEACH DEBATING AS A CORE SKILL, NOT A PERIPHERAL ACTIVITY.

The central importance of discussion and debate in real-world commerce, civic life and other areas of employment demands that speaking and debating are given a much higher profile in the English curriculum. Children taught how to conduct and take part in a formal discussion and debate are much less likely to become aggressive social media participants, difficult work colleagues or even poor parents.

11. TEACHING LISTENING IS AS IMPORTANT AS TEACHING SPEAKING.

Having a clear and agreed understanding in an English department about what 'listening' looks like in the English classroom is as important as knowing what to look for in effective speaking.

12. TEACH THE HISTORY OF THE ENGLISH LANGUAGE AS AN ENTITLEMENT.

From the beginning in secondary school, children should learn about the history of the English language and assimilate a simple timeline that includes all the most significant shifts in the language between the Roman invasion and today. By the time they reach 16, they should be able to recognise obvious examples of English from different historical periods without undue difficulty.

13. BUILD ALL ENGLISH WORK ON BASIC KNOWLEDGE ABOUT LINGUISTICS, ETYMOLOGY AND ORTHOGRAPHY.

Substantial time needs to be invested in the first two or three years of secondary school to study these three, key foundational areas of knowledge. The aim should be to give pupils a confident sense of how languages work and how English in particular fits into the wider pattern and global landscape. They need to think of etymology and orthography as the stable foundations, the prime rule sets, on which language is built and modified by time and usage.

14. TEACH HANDWRITING IN LESSON TIME.

It's inevitable that many children starting secondary school will not yet be adept at writing by hand. The sooner they gain a visible level of fluency, confidence and speed, the more likely they are to do justice to what they know and are learning in a wide range of subjects. Therefore, it's important all English teachers have some effective, agreed strategies for improving penmanship that can be used as necessary, without disrupting normal lessons and teaching. It's far better to expect this as a common problem than to think of it as an unusual weakness requiring additional resources or interventions.

15. DEVELOP THEIR ABILITY TO WRITE BY PROVOKING THEM TO THINK.

The relationship between thinking and writing should be spelled out to children. Reflective, pensive behaviour is not a natural consequence of growing up. Classroom lessons provide English teachers with a rich opportunity to use a wide variety of techniques they commonly share to provoke reflection and thought in all those they teach. It's easy to underestimate just how difficult it is for many children to put that first sentence together because they have simply never learned to focus on the blank page and think.

16. INCULCATE THE SCHOLARLY HABITS AND ATTITUDES TOWARDS LEARNING PER SE THAT PRODUCE LIFELONG READERS OF BOOKS.

Thinking of reading books in terms of reading levels is pointless because the tools widely used to assess the levels are far too crude to be of any educational value. Children need to appreciate the essential part books play in all scholarship and human endeavour. This means thinking especially carefully about the practical conditions through which you nurture reading, the physical spaces like the school library and the values about *learning* as a noun that you want children to absorb. The English department should be a dominant stakeholder in any school's library and make an unequivocal case for silent, concentrated reading as the foundation for all future learning and work.

17. CHOOSE ONE BOOK TO TEACH THEM TO BE SCHOLARLY READERS. IT'S HOW YOU TEACH IT THAT COUNTS. YOU DON'T NECESSARILY NEED BOOK LISTS.

It's worth questioning the idea that the more books you get a child to read, the quicker they'll progress in English. The real nature of the challenge is how to excite and engage children in *learning* successfully. The task at this stage is not to offer them a catalogue or reading list, but to create committed readers of books. It might take only one book to achieve this if it's taught well and what you do in the classroom makes scholarly practice look exciting and attractive.

18. TEACH POEMS AND NOVELS AS AESTHETIC AND CULTURALLY SIGNIFICANT ARTEFACTS TO BE ADMIRED AND ENJOYED IN THEIR OWN RIGHT, NOT PRIMARILY AS PROMPTS TO WRITTEN WORK BY PUPILS.

The English curriculum often positions important novels, poems and plays as exemplars. They are used to ignite children's own writing. This should be a secondary consideration and they should learn to see these kinds of texts as significant cultural artefacts with considerable historical and aesthetic value. They are far more likely to be able to talk or write well about any famous literary work if they have been encouraged simply to enjoy it. Reading for aesthetic pleasure is an absolute prerequisite for all English work.

19. TEACH POETRY AS THE STOCKADE EVERY CIVILISATION ERECTS AGAINST BARBARITY.

Poetry has a particularly important role to play in any real-world curriculum. It's where words and language are tested to their limits, and children can learn so much from poetry that has value in the real world. It teaches them, better than any other form, what words can and cannot do. The contemporary popular image of poetry as a self-indulgent, clique-ridden, arcane activity is only worsened by teaching that encourages children to write their own poetry as primarily an expressive activity, not a highly disciplined one. They should learn that understanding what great poets do with words only sharpens their own linguistic aptitude.

20. DESIGN A LINGUISTIC AND LITERARY TIMELINE.

In the way chemists rely on the periodic table, English teachers should all be able rely on a linguistic and literary timeline that display all the most important steps in the history of the English language and its literature. As children progress through secondary school, at any one point they should be able to see where the work they are doing sits on those timelines and understand how it relates to all the work they have previously done. They should have the opportunity to observe these timelines in parallel. There is no one definitive timeline, but it should not be too difficult for English departments to agree on the main steps and highlights in the history of the language and on who our most influential and famous authors have been. This shouldn't be a detailed exercise. What children need is a trustworthy frame of reference that relies on accurate chronology and scholarship.

21. WEAVE SPOKEN ENGLISH THROUGHOUT THE ENTIRE ENGLISH CURRICULUM, EMBRACING EVERYTHING FROM THE MOST PRACTICAL – HOW TO DELIVER AN EFFECTIVE PRESENTATION – TO THE MOST AESTHETIC – HOW TO LISTEN TO, READ AND ENJOY GREAT POETRY.

Oracy should not be treated as a last-minute requirement for an exam board. English teachers need to think of it as equal to writing as a formative assessment tool. This means they also need to explain that to children and create an expectation in them that what they say about a text or an idea under discussion is as important an indicator of their *learning* as what they write. The modern tendency some teachers have of disregarding dialect or accent, or of actively inviting children to share linguistic habits or trends, has no value or place in the real world. If English teaching fails to explain to children that the real world has expectations about language use that prioritise formality and clarity, that eschew individuality, then it's not just failing them but effectively handicapping them.

22. TEACHING LITERATURE IS INSEPARABLE FROM TEACHING ENGLISH.

Studying literature is not a nice-to-have, simply because some technocrat or 'here today; gone tomorrow' politician thinks it doesn't have the same cash value in the marketplace as maths. It's ineluctably linked to studying English because literature is where you find the best exponents of the English language. This implies a radical rethink both about the way English literature is formally examined and especially the way it's increasingly being marginalised as a secondary school subject.

23. ENGLISH DEPARTMENTS MUST ARTICULATE FOR THEMSELVES WHY THEY ARE ASKING PUPILS TO READ A COMPLETE NOVEL BEFORE EXPLAINING THOSE EXPECTATIONS TO THE CHILDREN EQUALLY CLEARLY.

Given that surveys and researchers are repeatedly reporting less and less time being spent by children reading books in private, it's vital that English teaching counters this external pressure and positions reading as central to all serious learning and scholarship. This suggests teachers should spend time explaining precisely to any group of children why it's expected they read any specific lengthy work of fiction or nonfiction. In the real world, you are competing for their time, and anything you can do to win that competition is worth doing.

24. HELP THEM TO SEE LITERATURE AS THE BEATING HEART OF DEMOCRATIC THOUGHT. IN THE LITERARY TIMELINE, THERE NEEDS TO BE A KEY THREAD TRACING FREEDOM OF EXPRESSION AND THE CRUCIAL ROLE SPECIFIC AUTHORS AND WORKS HAVE PLAYED IN ITS HISTORY.

Literature has a profound and significant relationship with the development of democracy that should be clearly visible in the literary timeline. Children should know, and be able to refer to, some of the most important literature that has had an impact on the development of real-world

democratic freedoms, and consequently value the democratic responsibilities waiting for them after school. That democracy relies on freedom
of expression is a real-world truth all English departments should teach.

25. BUILD THEIR LITERARY TOOLKIT. WHAT IS IT THAT YOU KNOW HOW TO DO AND WHICH YOU WANT THEM TO KNOW HOW TO DO TOO?

This is quite a substantial challenge and one that would benefit from
formal discussion with English teaching colleagues. Some of this will
be taught already, although it's likely to be done in an unstructured way
and rely very much on individual teachers' preferences. The key idea to
embrace is that it's worth investing some time in identifying specific
things – even if you start with summative exam syllabuses and work
backwards – that enhance their ability to write knowledgeably about the
texts they study. No exam syllabus I've ever seen does anything more than
scratch the surface of this challenge.

26. MAKE YOURSELF AN EXPERT IN ONLINE PROVENANCE.

The real-world prevalence of online material and resources aimed at teenagers means it's an absolute necessity that English teachers have expertise
in identifying new, valuable sources of information and knowledge about
literature, and recommending those they are already familiar with and
know well. This can't happen if teachers don't accept a responsibility to
maintain an interest in literary studies and research.

27. TEACH THEM ABOUT THE RISKS OF WRITING ONLINE.

It's highly likely that many pupils will already have at least one online
identity somewhere which involves them submitting text by the time they
start secondary school. They may have several identities like this, and
some may be at the heart of their closest friendships. If they aren't taught
about the risks in the context of their English studies, they will inevitably
come to regard this kind of writing as, in some magical way, immune
to all the other teaching about language they are subject to. They will
ultimately only add to the mountain of adults, many of them successful
professionals, who manage to completely divorce their online behaviour
from every other aspect of their social life and career. This is likely to be
impossible for many teachers who haven't as yet concerned themselves
unduly about the online world, or grasped that the word 'virtual' is just

another marketing tag and that this is very much a real-world, English teaching problem.

28. EDUCATE THEM NOT JUST ABOUT HOW TO USE THE ENGLISH LANGUAGE, BUT WHERE, WHY AND WHAT THE CONSEQUENCES MAY BE.

Again, for teachers who have only a limited interest in, or engagement with, online platforms, this implies a lot of additional work and learning for themselves. It is at least work that can be done individually as long as the responsibility is acknowledged, but it would also benefit from discussion with colleagues who may have more experience. Until such time as technology evolution slows down markedly, the onus is on teachers to keep abreast of at least the major platforms and their associated risks. But this isn't just a social media issue. What they need to know is that technology is likely to figure significantly every time they are required to write in the real world. It's vital they learn how to take that into account so that they're able to make informed – not deliberately engineered – choices.

29. DON'T INTRODUCE TECHNOLOGY FOR WRITING UNTIL THEY HAVE A CONFIDENT GRASP OF PERSONAL EXPRESSION WITHOUT IT.

With the exception of children with specific educational needs, fluent, confident handwriting has to precede writing with any kind of keyboard. This refers back to the very first point in this appendix: technology tends to constrain language use, not liberate it. Relying on a touchscreen or a keyboard before you have established a confidence writing by hand means that all manner of attention-grabbing incentives offered by the device or the software will disrupt your ability to turn thought into prose. Thinking and writing *by hand* remains a fundamental skill on which much of their future academic or career success is built.

30. REMOVE MOBILE PHONES FROM TEACHING SPACES COMPLETELY.

There are simply no convincing arguments for allowing mobile phones in classrooms. Even where their use is banned, their presence in a pocket or bag remains a powerful distraction few teenagers have the maturity to resist.

31. INSTIL A PROFOUND SENSE OF LINGUISTIC INTEGRITY.

By far the weightiest conclusion I reached in researching and writing this book is the belief that, precisely because the impact of technology on English has been ubiquitous, those who teach it now have a hugely important and new role to play in society. They have been forced into a position where, if they don't embrace the role as defenders of the English language, there is no one else with the knowledge or skills to do so – and the consequences we all face is an even faster slide into a real world where increasing numbers of words are already Humptys' playthings, and the ability to communicate for all of us is consequently eroded. The implications for debate, free speech and ultimately democracy could not be more extreme. Children must learn today that the English language is a rich and powerful gift, not a toy. That just as humanity has finally recognised there is no planet B, there is no language that cannot be corrupted, no word that cannot be usurped, no form of communication free from pollution. They must understand we are all stewards of the language we share, then go out and tend it in the real world.

SELECT BIBLIOGRAPHY

Beck, Isabel, L., McKeown, Margaret, G., and Kucan, Linda. (2013). *Bringing Words to Life*, Guildford Publications.

Carr, Nicholas, (2011). *The Shallows*, Atlantic Books.

Clements, James, (2017). *Teaching English by the Book*, Routledge.

Cox, Bob, Crawford, Leah, Jones, Verity., (2019) *Opening Doors to a Richer English Curriculum for Ages 10 to 13*, Crown House Publishing.

Cuban, Larry, (2003). *Oversold and Underused: Computers in the Classroom*, Harvard University Press.

De Bruyckere, Pedro, Kirschner, Paul A, and Hulshof, Casper D., (2015). *Urban Myths about Learning and Education*, Academic Press.

Goldthorpe, John., Bukodi, Erzsébet., (2018). *Social Mobility and Education in Britain: Research, Politics and Policy*, CUP.

Hirsch, E.D., (2016). *Why Knowledge Matters*, Harvard Educational Publishing.

Lemov, Doug, Driggs Colleen and Woolway, Erica., (2016). *Reading Reconsidered*, Jossey Bass.

Murray, Douglas, (2019. *The Madness of Crowds*, Bloomsbury Continuum.

Murphy, James, Ed., (2019). *The researchED Guide to Literacy. An Evidence-informed Guide for Teachers*, John Catt Educational Ltd.

Murphy, James & Murphy Diane, (2018). *Thinking Reading: What every secondary teacher needs to know about reading*, John Catt Educational Ltd.

Myatt, Mary, (2018) *The Curriculum: Gallimaufry to coherence*, John Catt Educational Ltd.

Postman, Neil, (2011). *Amusing Ourselves to Death*, Penguin.

Quigley, Alex, (2018). *Closing the Vocabulary Gap*, Routledge.

Robinson, Martin, (2019). *Curriculum: Athena Versus the Machine*, Crown House Publishing.

Standish, Alex and Sehgal Cuthbert, Alka, (2017). *What Schools Should Teach*, UCL IoE Press.

Williams, James, (2018). *Stand Out of Our Light*, Cambridge University Press.

Willingham, Daniel T., (2010). *Why Don't Students Like School?*, John Wiley and Sons.

Willingham, Daniel T., (2017). *The Reading Mind: A Cognitive Approach to Understanding How the Mind Reads,* Jossey Bass.

Wolf, Maryanne., (2008). *Proust and the Squid,* Icon Books Ltd.

Wolf, Maryanne., (2018). *Reader, Come Home: The Reading Brain in a Digital World,* Harper.